SECRET
FLORENCE

Niccolò Rinaldi

PHOTOGRAPHS
Waris Grifi

JONGLEZ PUBLISHING

travel guides

Niccolò Rinaldi, born in Florence in 1962, was the UN representative for information in Afghanistan, adjunct secretary general, european parliament deputy, and elected in the Central Italian Collegiate (which includes Florence.) He has written travel books and corresponding works on central Asia, Africa, and florentine travelers.

We have taken great pleasure in drawing up *Secret Florence* and hope that through its guidance you will, like us, continue to discover unusual, hidden or little-known aspects of the city.

Descriptions of certain places are accompanied by thematic sections highlighting historical details or anecdotes as an aid to understanding the city in all its complexity.

Secret Florence also draws attention to the multitude of details found in places that we may pass every day without noticing. These are an invitation to look more closely at the urban landscape and, more generally, a means of seeing our own city with the curiosity and attention that we often display while travelling elsewhere …

Comments on this guidebook and its contents, as well as information on places we may not have mentioned, are more than welcome and will enrich future editions..

Don't hesitate to contact us:
E-mail: info@jonglezpublishing.com
Jonglez Publishing
25 rue du Maréchal Foch
78000 Versailles, France

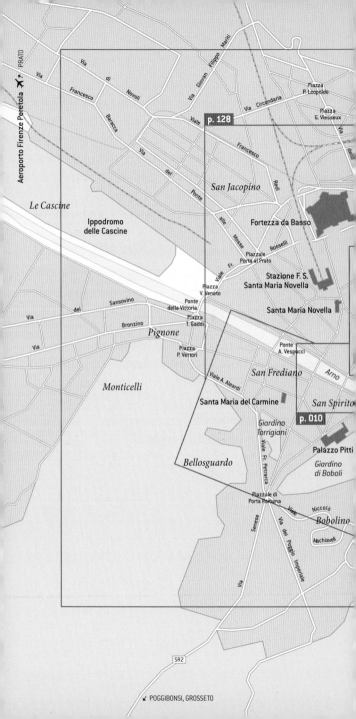

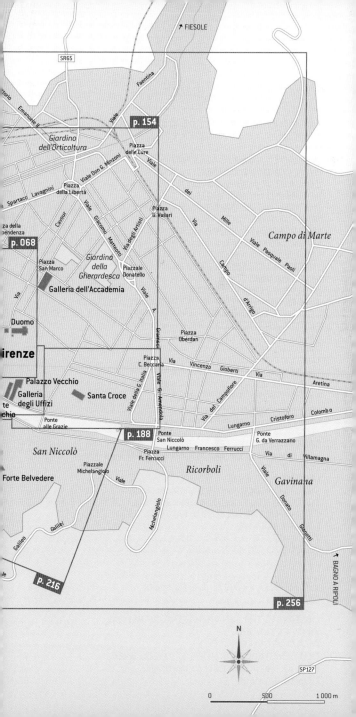

CONTENTS

Piazza della Signoria

Duomo / San Lorenzo

Santa Maria Novella

CONTENTS

SS Annunziata

Santa Croce

Oltrarno

Outskirts of Florence

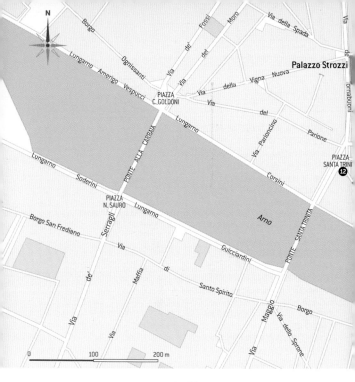

Piazza della Signoria

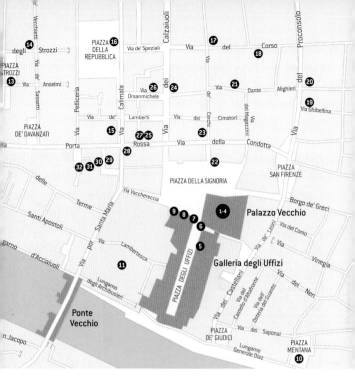

THE ALCHEMICAL SYMBOLS IN THE STUDIOLO

The Alchemical Laboratory of Francesco I de' Medici

Palazzo Vecchio

Francesco I de' Medici (Florence, 25 March 1541 – Florence, 19 October 1587) commissioned a special *Studiolo* (study) within the Palazzo Vecchio. The decoration was in part the work of the most famous Mannerist painter of the day, Giorgio Vasari, who was commissioned to oversee the entire project (1570 - 1572), with the assistance of the humanist scholars Giovanni Battista Adriani and Vincenzo Borghini. The *Studiolo* is actually divided into two parts: a study proper and an alchemical laboratory, the latter being a sort of *wunderkammer* in which Francesco I, who had little taste for politics, often took refuge. The prince would here engage in alchemical experiments or else delight in his collection of rare objects, all within a space that was decorated with a series of large-format paintings from his collection. The walls were, in fact, adorned with thirty-four paintings, mainly of religious or mythological themes. Other works included Mirabello Cavalori's *Wool Workshop* and Giovanni Battista Naldini's *Allegory of Dreams*, which undoubtedly reflects the interior of Francesco's nearby bedchamber. Pride of place went to a portrait of the duke's mother, Eleonora of Toledo, painted by Bronzino. As already mentioned, the *Studiolo* became a place of refuge for Francesco, a man of complex and taciturn character. Soon after his death, his brother and heir, Ferdinando I, had the place dismantled (1590) – so completely that all trace of it disappeared. However, in the twentieth century it was "reassembled" after surviving traces of the ceiling frescoes made it possible for Giovanni Poggi (Superintendent of the Cultural Heritage in Tuscany) and Alfredo Lesni (Head of the Florence City Arts Department) to identify the original room in 1910. Miraculously, it was possible to restore the thirty-four paintings that had decorated the walls, together with eight sculptures in bronze. Part of Francesco I's commission to Vasari for his *Studiolo* was for paintings of the four natural elements (Earth, Water, Fire and Air), upon which alchemists worked whilst pursing their explorations of Natural Philosophy within their laboratories; those laboratories themselves were, in fact, a symbol of the alchemical universe, a place of both Prayer and Work (*ora et labora*), a *laboratorium* and a laboratory. It is, however, unlikely that Francesco I actually performed alchemical experiments here; the place is much better suited to the reading of alchemical texts, with Francesco not venturing beyond the sphere of intellectual or theoretical alchemy (see page opposite). However, the duke has left us a precious collection of paintings inspired by the theme of alchemical practice – in particular, the ceiling decoration of *Prometeo che riceve i gioelli della Natura* (Prometheus Receiving the Jewels of Nature). Painted in 1570 by Francesco Poppi, this work shows Nature bestowing upon Prometheus the "quintessence" necessary for the creation of the Philosopher's Stone. The image symbolises the creation of the Perfect Man, who is endowed with a Spirit enlightened by the Flame of Reason – the torch of which is associated with both Prometheus and Lucifer. Another work, this time by Vasari, depicts *Perseus and Andromeda*, the Greek myth which alchemists took to symbolise the hermetist disciple (embodied by Perseus) triumphing over the deficiencies of his lower nature (and over vanity in particular). As a result of this victory, the disciple is able to use the sword of true justice to free himself and hence reveal the higher, immortal nature of his soul (represented by Andromeda). The 1572 painting of *Atalanta and Hippomenes* by Sebastiano Marsili symbolises the disciple pursuing the primary material for the alchemical *Magnum Opus*, a theme which was the starting-point of a treatise on alchemy written in 1617 by the German alchemist Michael Maier (1568 - 1622) with the Latin title *Atalanta fugiens* (Atalanta in Flight). Hence, this association was a standard of Renaissance Hermetism. Francesco I's reputation is such that it is difficult to argue that he possessed the virtues required of a true disciple of alchemical philosophy. On the contrary, he is remembered as a despot. Whilst Cosimo I (who was also interested in alchemy) had managed to preserve Florence's independence, Francesco behaved as a vassal of the Habsburg Holy Roman Emperor, imposing taxes upon his subjects in order to pay substantial sums into the imperial coffers. It is even said that his death was due to poisoning.

Alchemy

Most religious orders of the Middle Ages and the Renaissance considered *alchemy* (from the Coptic term *Allah-Chemia*, or divine chemistry) as the *Art of the Holy Spirit* or *Royal Art* of the divine creation of the world and man. It was connected to Orthodox Catholic doctrine.

The followers of this art divided it into two principal forms. *Spiritual alchemy* exclusively concerns the inspiration of the soul, transforming the impure elements of the body in the refined states of spiritual consciousness, which is also called the *Way of the Repentants*. *Laboratory alchemy*, called the *Way of the Philosophers*, reproduces the alchemical universe of the transmutation of nature's impure elements into noble metals, such as silver and gold, in the laboratory. These two alchemical practices are generally followed in combination, thus becoming the *Way of the Humble*, where the humility is that of man faced with the grandeur of the universe reproduced in the laboratory (in Latin *labor + oratorium*); the alchemy of the (interior) soul is expressed exteriorly in the laboratory. Those who practise *Laboratory alchemy* with the sole purpose of finding silver and gold, and thus neglect the essential aspects of the betterment of the soul, will fail and become *charlatans*, who might have a wide-ranging culture but certainly not the required moral qualities. To avoid becoming a *charlatan* (it was this heretic form that was condemned by the Church), followers must balance the heart and soul, culture and moral qualities, penitence and humility, to become a true philosopher.

SEARCHING FOR A MYSTERIOUS FRESCO BY LEONARDO DA VINCI

Lost or hidden?

Salone dei Cinquecento - Palazzo Vecchio
Piazza della Signoria
Open October–March every day except Thursday from 9am to 7pm, Thursday
9am to 2pm; April–September every day except Thursday from 9am to 11pm,
Thursday 9am to 2pm
Closed New Year's Day, Easter Sunday, May 1, August 15 and December 25

The *Salone dei Cinquecento* was the main chamber in the Palazzo Vecchio, and today it poses a real enigma. We know that the magistrates of the city commissioned Leonardo da Vinci to paint a fresco in this council chamber, and that the artist did produce a work depicting *The Battle of Anghiari*, but that fresco has now disappeared, leaving no trace. A real mystery: a fresco – and by Leonardo da Vinci to boot – that was once located in a specific place, right in the heart of Florentine government, and yet it seems to have vanished into thin air! Experts have long been divided between two explanations. For the most part, art historians say that the fresco must have been done on plaster that dried too quickly, and this would explain why it deteriorated beyond repair. So, when Vasari was commissioned to redecorate the hall, he decided to paint over the previous fresco. Another, smaller, group of experts indignantly rejects the very notion that Leonardo did not know the basic techniques of fresco painting, also arguing that Vasari would not have dared lay hands upon the work of a master artist he admired above all others. Their hypothesis is

that a second brick wall was built just a few centimetres in front of the fresco, in order to preserve it; all you have to do in order to admire Leonardo's work is demolish the wall with Vasari's fresco.

Given sophisticated new methods of restoration, you might think it would be possible to resolve this matter. Even without confirmation, the supporters of the second thesis are so confident of the survival of Leonardo's fresco that they argue there is a reference to it in Vasari's own work: if you look carefully at one of the standards that appear in the latter fresco you see it bears the words *Cerca, Trova* [Look, Find].

THE UFO OF PALAZZO VECCHIO   ③

Fifteenth-century Ufology

Palazzo Vecchio
Piazza della Signoria
Open October–March every day except Thursday from 9am to 7pm, Thursday
9am to 2pm; April–September every day except Thursday from 9am to 11pm,
Thursday 9am to 2pm
Closed New Year's Day, Easter Sunday, May 1, August 15 and December 25

A room on the top floor of Palazzo Vecchio has long attracted particular interest from Ufologists and all those who argue for the existence of extraterrestrial life forms – or, indeed, from those who have simply heard about a Renaissance painting which is unique of its kind, apparently depicting a spaceship piloted by Martians. The fifteenth-century painting is actually in a form reminiscent of a flying saucer, as it is a tondo measuring 1 metre in diameter. There were many paintings in this form at the time, but there is a peculiar detail in this work. The subject matter itself is the traditional depiction of *The Virgin and Child with St John the Baptist*, but in the background the shepherd and his dog are not watching over their flocks but rather craning their necks to look up into the sky. And when you follow their line of sight, you see a strange circular object, painted in such a way to give the impression it is rotating, or at least moving. To cap it all, the lower part of this curious grey-coloured "spaceship" seems to be surrounded by an aureole of spherical bodies, whilst the upper part bristles with projecting rods that resemble of antennas. Looking at it nowadays, you would swear that this was a UFO – perhaps seen by the person commissioning the work, who then asked the artist (undoubtedly a pupil of Filippo Lippi) to "document" it. While all this may seem highly improbable, it only took one architect to draw attention to this feature of the work (in 1978) for this painting to be raised to iconic status. It immediately underwent pains-

taking restoration and was subjected to sophisticated analysis both in Italy and the United States, in order to rule out the possibility of the "UFO" being a hoax created by later additions. However, the enigma has yet to be resolved. Why are the shepherd and his dog looking at this strange object in the sky? And why was that object included here? Think what you will, there is no denying that the presence of this fifteenth-century spaceship has been a real boon for this undoubtedly minor painting.

PATROLLING THE CITY FROM ABOVE④

An itinerary over 40 metres above ground level

Open October–March every day except Thursday from 10am to 5pm, Thursday 10am to 2pm; April–September every day except Thursday from 9am to 11pm, Thursday 9am to 2pm
Reservations required, admission free; Tel: Monday–Sunday, 055 2768224 from 9.30am to 4.30pm or e-mail info.museoragazzi@comune.fi.it
Visits should normally take place between 11.30am and 3pm, any day of the week
www.palazzovecchio-museoragazzi.it
Warning: there are architectural barriers difficult for those of limited mobility

Palazzo Vecchio never ceases to amaze visitors, offering a wide range of visits and tours. After the launch of a tour designed for young people (Museo dei Ragazzi), another recent addition is the reopening of the patrol route used by guards as they did their rounds to watch over the city and protect the palace – the seat of government – from possible attack. Running around the entire palazzo – that is, offering a 360° view over the city – this route is located over 40 metres above street level, with a series of windows providing panoramic views over different parts of the city. There are other more conventional places where you can see Florence from above – the Parnassus Garden in Via Trento, Forte Belvedere, Fiesole, Villa Bardini, Piazzale Michelangelo, the Rose Garden – but the charm of this one is that, like the top of the church of Orsanmichele or the cupola of the Duomo, it offers a view of the city from within the urban fabric itself. Apart from the stunning views, this patrol route is also fascinating from an architectural point of view: it is unique in Florence in that it has not been changed since the Middle Ages, remaining just as Arnolfo di Cambio designed it. While various other parts of the palazzo were being modified over the centuries, nobody turned their attention to this elevated route. Perhaps it was just too high up and too "military" in character – even for the extensive modifications carried out under Giorgio Vasari in the sixteenth century.

Machiolations for the hot oil treatment

At various points along the patrol route you see openings that were intended for pouring boiling oil over attackers. Now glazed over, these machiolations offer a view of Piazza della Signoria that will take your breath away.

CONTINI BONACOSSI COLLECTION

Hidden store of masterpieces tucked away in the Uffizi

Via Lambertesca, 4
www.uffizi.firenze.it
Admission free, but only on request
Tel: 055 238 8809 or info.uffizi@polomuseale.firenze.it

Everyone hurries to the Uffizi; the excellence and abundance of its artistic wealth are enough to quench any thirst for culture. However, in the rooms adjacent to the great museum a small gem is tucked away, generally ignored even by the better-informed tourist. This is the Contini Bonacossi Bequest, which became part of the Uffizi in 1998: a miniature museum in itself, it comprises thirty-five paintings of excellent quality which were all chosen with great care and discernment by Count and Countess Contini Bonacossi, with expert advice from the art historian Roberto Longhi. Away from the hurly-burly of the main galleries, these rooms have an almost private feel to them. Here, you can enjoy a large number of terracotta and faience pieces by the Della Robbia Pottery, masterpieces by Sassetta and Bernini, a small selec-

tion of Spanish works (Goya, Velazquez, Zurbaran and El Greco) and works by various Venetian masters (Bellini, Veronese, Tintoretto, Jacopo da Bassano, Cima da Conegliano and Paolo Veneziano). There is also a fresco by Andrea del Castagno, an altarpiece by Cimabue and a Virgin by Bramantino. In any other city, a gallery of this quality would be ranked as a prestigious museum in its own right. But in Florence – and within the immediate shadow of the Uffizi it has to be content with the rank of unusual and little-known collection, a sort of back-up squad of masterpieces. However, this is no reason to ignore it – on the contrary.

Contini Bonacossi Collection: a difficult bequest

The Contini Bonacossi Collection, bequeathed to the Italian state in 1969 and now open to the public, contains only a small part of the large number of works of art amassed by Count Alessandro Contini Bonacossi (1878 - 1955), entrepreneur and collector, and his wife Vittoria Galli.

In 1945, the Contini Bonacossi spouses had expressed their wish to leave the entire collection (1,066 works, including paintings, drawings, sculptures, ceramics, furniture and contemporary works of art) to a public institution, provided the collection was kept intact. Although the Vatican had initially been approached, the Italian state was finally chosen. The bequest was not straightforward: the legalities dragged on for decades, during which time details even appeared in legal columns in the press.

On the count's death in 1955, the details had not yet been finalised: some of his heirs opposed the bequest, while others supported it.

This controversy between some of the heirs and the state was only defused in 1969, through an ad hoc legal decree signed by President Giuseppe Saragat. It was established that the state would obtain some works (ultimately thirty-five) free of charge for several Florentine museums, which were to be designated by a specially constituted commission of experts.

In return, the heirs were to keep the rest of the collection, with the additional right to sell pieces abroad, and the withdrawal of an export ban for twelve years. Many works of art were thus sold to private individuals and other museums, including the Uffizi, which bought *Saint Monica with Two Children* by Paolo Uccello, Loren-

zo Lotto's *Suzanna and the Elders* and *the Resurrection of Christ* attributed to Titian.

This dispersal of the original collection provoked a reaction on the part of the authorities: questions were raised in parliament and legal proceedings were initiated against several heirs and some members of the commission of experts. The issue was only resolved in 1979, with the full acquittal of all the parties involved.

BOTHERING MICHELANGELO

The talent of a genius

Palazzo Vecchio
Piazza della Signoria

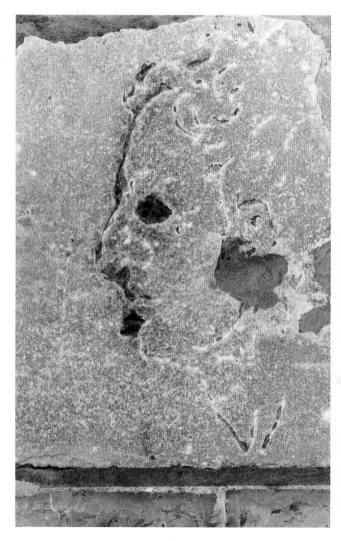

To the right of the main entrance to Palazzo Vecchio stands the statue of Hercules and Cacus; behind that sculpture – just above the bench now used by tourists – you can see the most famous work of antique "graffiti" in the whole of Florence. Look closely to make out the outline of a face – a sketch portrait that is attributed to Michelangelo himself. As might be expected, the story behind this original work carved "straight into the stone" is itself original.

However, as is often the case with stories regarding works that have become part of popular tradition, there are two – contradictory – versions of that tale.

The first says that Michelangelo was constantly being pestered by someone who insisted on telling him rambling and irrelevant stories. One day, when the artist had his hammer and chisel handy, he carved this bore's portrait into the corner of the palazzo while pretending to listen, which would explain why the Florentines still refer to the figure in this carving as *L'Importuno.*

The second version has it that Michelangelo was here when he saw a convict brought for execution in front of the palazzo. Struck by the criminal's expression, he decided to try and capture it before the man was executed.

As he had so little time – and didn't want to take his eyes off his "subject" – the only solution was to carve the image directly into the stone at shoulder height behind him. This would explain why the image is only sketched in, even if the artist has managed to capture the man's appearance; the very economy of means bears witness to Michelangelo's remarkable talent.

You decide which story you like best. What is beyond doubt is that this little masterpiece, carved into the wall of a busy public place, still gives rise to debate ... and still attracts the attention of passers-by.

MICHAEL ANGELVS BONAROTVS PATRITIVS
FLORENTINVS AN AGENS LXXII

QVANTVM IN NATVRA ARS NATVRAQVE POSSIT IN ARTE
HIC QVI NATVRÆ PAR FVIT ARTE DOCET

M D XLVI

THE REMAINS OF THE CHURCH OF SAN PIER SCHERAGGIO

"Inside these walls the voice of Dante echoed within the people's councils"

Via della Ninna

San Pier Scheraggio takes less time to visit than any other church in Florence, though what you are visiting is not so much a church as the remains of a church. But these ruins are not tucked away somewhere or buried underground; they are there in plain sight. In Via della Ninna, almost opposite the main entrance to Palazzo Vecchio, you will find – against a wall of the Uffizi – two large arches surmounting elegant columns. The whole has been bricked in on the Uffizi side and is now disfigured by the presence of two windows. Furthermore, when you look down through some grates, you can also see the foundation of the church, whose presence here is commemorated by a discreet plaque. The inscription relates a very special detail about San Pier Scheraggio: *Tra le cui mura nei consigli di popolo sonò la voce di Dante* ["within whose walls, Dante's voice rang out in the people's councils"]. Built around the year 1000, the church stood near Dante's house, not far from Piazza della Signoria, and it is likely that the citizens of Florence gathered here in assembly during the more tumultuous periods in the city's history. The place also possessed some fine works of art; Cimabue, for example, painted the frescoes in one of the naves. Unfortunately, San Pier Scheraggio was very badly – that is, too well – located. In 1298, the Cimabue was demolished for building work on the Palazzo della Signoria or Palazzo dei Priori [Priors] as it was known as the time.

When the Uffizi was built in the sixteenth century, the extant remains of the church were again in the way, so they had to be demolished. The one exception was part of a nave, which Vasari converted into a room that still makes up part of the ground floor of the Uffizi. For a reason that is now unknown, these two arches, complete with their columns, were spared and incorporated within the wall. Nowadays giving the impression of a trompe-l'oeil architectural composition or "quotation", these few remnants are clear proof that this "city of many layers" still preserves some of its very earliest stones.

"EMERGENCY EXIT" IN VIA DELLA NINNA

⑧

Saving the Duke of Athens

Via della Ninna

In Via della Ninna, along the side of Palazzo Vecchio, there is an unusually small door, very low and almost square. This was the famous "emergency exit" built for Gualtieri VI di Brienne, the "Duke of Athens" who tyrannised Florence from 1342 to 1343 and was scorned by the Florentines for his brutality.

Aware of the many conspiracies against him, the duke had a secret passage built inside the palazzo, which led to this door, to give him direct and discreet access to the street. The tyrant was indeed perceptive, for this was precisely how he escaped in July 1343, following a popular uprising which called for the restoration of citizens' rights.

> The name Via della Ninna derives from *ninna nanna* (lullaby), because the church of San Pier Scheraggio (named after the schiaraggio, or drain that ran beside the city walls) once had an image of the Virgin holding the Sleeping Child in her arms.

SELF-PORTRAIT BY BENVENUTO CELLINI

The grimacing creator of Perseus

Loggia dei Lanzi
Piazza della Signoria

Gazing ahead proudly as he holds out the bleeding severed head of Medusa, Benvenuto Cellini's *Perseus* is a powerful and dramatic figure. However, this is a "double" work of art, in the sense that the apparent image also contains another. To discover this, you have to go right into the Loggia dei Lanzi. (The name is derived from *lanzichenecchi*, the Italian version of the German term *landsknecht*, referring to the Lutheran mercenaries who camped out in this loggia prior to the Sack of Rome in 1527). At the back of the statue, note how the carefully rendered musculature in the nape of the neck forms a human face. This is the self-portrait of Cellini himself, with a grimace that would definitely have been considered out of place on a monumental statue. Whether a joke at his own or his public's expense, this is a detail that your children (or friends) will be delighted to discover.

Inside the Loggia dei Lanzi, other curiosities are waiting to be discovered: the great arches of the vault rest on capitals without columns, as if they were directly hung on the wall, supported by winged putti and female figures, giving the structure a feeling of astonishing lightness. Below these suspended capitals are hooks for hanging the tapestries used to decorate the Loggia at festival time. Two plaques in the Loggia are worth a look. One of them traces the various stages of Italian unification. The other, which has a Latin inscription, recalls that Florence changed its calendar in 1750 so that New Year's Day was fixed on January 1, replacing the age-old tradition whereby the Florentine New Year fell on March 25.

Munich's Loggia

There is an almost identical replica of the Loggia dei Lanzi in Munich: the Feldernhalle, which dates back to the nineteenth century. Its dimensions are about the same, with three large arches and two lions, one on either side of the entrance steps, and an open space for sculptures.

The Loggia dei Lanzi owes its name to the German mercenaries known as *lansquenets* (Italian: *lanzichenecchi*). The cornice of the lateral entablature testifies to their presence. You can see the marks of musket balls from their firing practice (or when they'd drunk too much!) near the lions' heads carved directly in the *pietra dura*, another curiosity of the piazza.

March 25: the old Florentine New Year

On the right wall of the Loggia de' Lanzi, a plaque inscribed in Latin commemorates the entry into force of a Grand Ducal Decree of 1749, which established that henceforth the calendar year would begin on January 1.

Since late antiquity, the New Year had been celebrated on different dates in various European regions. For the Romans, it was a long-standing tradition that March was the first month of the year (hence the first astrological sign of the zodiac, the ram, begins on March 21), whereas the year began on March 1 in Venice, December 25 in the Papal States and March 25 in Florence.

With the introduction in 1582 of the Gregorian calendar, the solar dating system now in general use, in order to standardise the existing calendars it was established that New Year's Day should be taken as January 1, although this decision was not adopted everywhere.

Florence, for example, continued to start the calendar year on March 25. This date had great religious significance for the city: it was "Lady Day", the Christian celebration of the announcement by the angel Gabriel to the Virgin Mary that she would conceive (a feast that originates from an ancient pagan tradition linked to the Revival of Nature in spring).

The Florentines were particularly devoted to Mary, even dedicating a Marian temple to the Holy Annunciation, in the square of the same name (Santissima Annunziata). It was not until November 1749 that the Grand Duke of Tuscany, Francis III of Lorraine, de-

cided that it was time to standardise the Florentine and Gregorian calendars, thus beginning the year on January 1. This last reform was also needed to coordinate the calendars within the Grand Duchy itself.

Although in Florence and Siena the year indeed began on March 25, that is to say, two months and twenty-four days later than modern usage, in Pisa and on the Tuscan coast the year always began on March 25, but nine months and seven days earlier than the "modern style" (according to the "Pisa" dating system). Although in Florence March 25 was the first day of 1748, in Pisa the same date of March 25 marked the end of 1748.

The grand-ducal reform also concerned the town clocks. It was decreed that public clocks would be set according to the French standard, dividing the days into twice twelve hours (day and night) and no longer into twenty-four.

The count started from midnight rather than from the hour after sunset, as had been the case until then.

So you can see in Piazza della Signoria itself, on Palazzo Vecchio's Arnolfo tower, a twelve-hour clock with its distinctive single pointer, designed by mathematician Vincenzio Viviani in 1667.

The measurement of time, which at the outset was only acoustic (signalled by church bells), was as it happens inaugurated on March 25 1353.

AN EXCURSION ON THE ARNO WITH THE *RENAIOLI*

To see Florence from an unusual point of view

Arno embankment; access from Piazza Mentana
From late May to late September
Tel: 3477982356
www.renaioli.it

Having restored some of their boats, the *renaioli* are once more to be seen on the river Arno, powering their boats by means of the traditional asta – a pole similar to that used by the fishermen of African lagoons. You can book excursions along the river which provide a very unusual view of Florence.

The fullest trip starts at the barrier that is located beneath Piazza Mentana, just before the historic premises of the Canottieri Ponte Vecchio [Ponte Vecchio Rowing Club], the perfect place to have an aperitif beforehand or – on the terrace of the club – enjoy dinner afterwards. The *renaioli* take you in front of the loggia of the Uffizi and then under the arches of Ponte Vecchio, offering you the chance to see the historic houses perched on the bridge from beneath. The trip continues in the direction of the Santa Trinità bridge – affording a very unusual view of the piers of the central arch – and then as far as Ponte alla Carraia, without however venturing too close to the water barrage just before Ponte alla Vittoria. On the return trip, you pass close by the church "lapped by the Arno" – that is, San Jacopo, the apse of which rises up from the river itself.

Who are the Renaioli *?*

Renaioli are "sand gatherers" (rena = sand) – or rather the descendants of those who for centuries used to collect the river sand that played such a part in the building of Florentine palazzi. These tough workers were not the only ones whose boats were to be seen on the Arno: right up to the Second World War, the river was home to barges carrying merchandise or providing floating stages for performances, and of course there were pleasure craft. However, the *renaioli* were undoubtedly the only ones who were still working the river at the time of the terrible flood in November 1966. For centuries, these figures scrambled to sift through the sand immediately below the Ponte Vecchio,

which might contain precious waste from the goldsmiths' shops above. Furthermore, during the Fascist period, this was one of the few jobs open to the regime's opponents, given that you did not need a party membership card to be a renaiolo. After the war it was *renaioli* who eventually (in 1961) recovered the head of the statue of *Spring*, which had still been missing when the Ponte Santa Trinita was rebuilt after its destruction by the Wehrmacht.

The remarkable Ponte Vecchio

The Ponte Vecchio is like a mini-city suspended between the two banks of the Arno. One of its distinctive features is an ancient meridian, to the right of the monument dedicated to Benvenuto Cellini. Along the Vasari corridor you can also see the central panoramic windows that Mussolini had opened up during Hitler's visit to Florence in 1939, so that the two dictators could admire the setting sun from a privileged viewpoint. At the point where the bridge touches the shores of the Oltrarno district, the corridor deviates from its path and skirts the Torre Mannelli, which the owners had refused to demolish. And the two bricked-up doorways a few steps farther along the corridor were part of a private house that was incorporated into the construction. Unlike the Mannellis, some citizens were ready to sell out to accommodate Vasari's building work. The church of Santa Felicità is linked to the corridor by a small secret balcony with a slatted window, which allowed the Grand Duke and his wife to attend Mass safely and unobtrusively.

STAIRCASE OF SANTO STEFANO AL PONTE CHURCH

Treasures of Santo Stefano al Ponte

Piazza di Santo Stefano, 5
Tel: 055 217418
info@santostefanoalponte.it
www.santostefanoalponte.it

The former church of Santo Stefano al Ponte – damaged during the Second World War and by the 1966 flood, then deconsecrated in 1986 – has been converted into a multimedia exhibition space and concert hall that is home to the Orchestra Regionale Toscana. The church is named after the little piazza where it was built, less than 100 m from Ponte Vecchio.

This church was administered for centuries by Augustine friars from the Congregation of Lecceto, near Siena. Its original three aisles were merged into a single nave during a radical conversion in the seventeenth century at the initiative of Marquis Anton Maria Bartolommei, who had new and imposing decorations added in Florentine Baroque style. The marquis, who lived nearby, had proclaimed himself protector and patron of the church. His involvement resulted in some very original architecture with no curved surfaces at all. Indeed, the presence of unusual geometric and architectural figures creates a play of light and shadow which gives a sensation of dynamism and movement, despite the lack of rounded edges: instead of a circle, a dodecahedron; instead of an arch,

a half-dodecahedron; and instead of a curved base, niches and a segmented dome. According to one hypothesis, Marquis Bartolommei was inspired by Galileo's theory, which he greatly admired, that the divine is represented by geometric forms (the circle, for example) whose accuracy can only be gauged by experimentation and approximation using the broken lines of multifaceted spheres.

The interior holds other artistic treasures inside the interior: over the centuries, the churchSanto Stefano has typically received furniture and ornaments from other deconsecrated churches, San Pier Schieraggio for example, which was demolished to make way for the Uffizi, and Santa Cecilia, among others that were undergoing renovation.

Among these legacies is the splendid balustraded staircase, a masterpiece designed by Bernardo Buontalenti (1574) for Santa Trinita that was removed when the basilica was restored in Gothic style towards the end of the nineteenth century. The steps are edged with sculpted forms resembling open shells (or bat wings) that break up the outline.

Another masterpiece is the main altar by Giambologna (1594), originally in the church of Santa Maria Nuova.

Until 1986, in Santo Stefano al Ponte, notably in the sacristy, the Goldsmiths' Chapel and the adjoining convent complex, as had been the case for centuries, works of art were brought here from churches where Mass was no longer celebrated. These works formed the nucleus of the Diocesan Museum, which is now open to the public.

THE "MESSAGES" IN PALAZZO BARTOLINI SALIMBENI

"It is easier to criticise than to imitate"

Palazzo Bartolini Salimbeni
Piazza Santa Trinità, 1

Completed in 1532, this palazzo would give rise to controversy. In his designs, the architect Baccio d'Agnolo had shown a certain nonchalant daring; as is clear from the details of the façade, he had been more than happy to indulge the new taste for manifest echoes of the classical past. This building thus marked the advent within the city of the "Roman" style of Renaissance architecture, a style which may have been a hybrid but was not without its elegance. Vasari described Palazzo Bartolini Salimbeni as the "first in which one saw the windows adorned with pediments and the doorway accompanied by columns supporting an architrave, frieze and cornice". However, characteristic features of Florentine architecture were not totally omitted; look, for example, at the bench projecting from the bottom of the façade at street level. Still, that façade is noteworthy primarily for its unusual decorative columns and its triangular tympana. Overall, the design was taken as an attack upon the tastes prevailing in the Florence of the day – so much so that, just as happens nowadays, there was no lack of criticism and sarcasm. "This innovation," Vasari wrote, "would draw upon him [Baccio d'Agnolo] the censure of the Florentines, who overwhelmed him with mockery and satirical sonnets. He was scolded for having made a temple instead of a palazzo. This sarcasm so depressed Baccio that he almost lost his wits; however, he soon passed on to other things, thinking that the course he was following was the right one." If he did soon "pass on to other things", the criticism made such an impression upon the architect that he had the Latin inscription *Carpere promptus quam imitari* "it is easier to criticise than to imitate" engraved in plain view over the main doorway. And he would be proved right: his style was reassessed – and even imitated – with the advent of Mannerism.

Wide awake

The desire to communicate a message can be seen on other parts of this façade: another, more enigmatic inscription - *Per non dormire* [In order not to sleep] - appears over certain of the windows. Given that this motto comes from a family of wealthy merchants like the Bartolini Salimbeni, this might be taken this to be an exhortation to work – perhaps an allusion to the habit of getting to markets and auctions first in order to acquire the best merchandise. The cornice is also decorated with three poppies, the family emblem. Given the somniferous properties of the opium associated with this flower, some have seen this as another allusion to sleep.

SALA MARAINI

The Far East in Piazza Strozzi

Gabinetto Scientifico Letterario G.P. Vieusseux
Piazza Strozzi, 1
Tel: 055 288342
Visits on request Monday, Wednesday and Friday from 9am to 1.30pm;
Thursday 9am to 6pm

While the Sala Maraini may only be a room in a library, it has a very special atmosphere.

This collection of material relating to the Orient was put together by the Florence-born traveller, ethnologist and Orientalist Fosco Maraini (1912–2004) and comprises a collection of 70,000 photographs and more than 8,000 books (most of the publications so rare that they are only found here).

The library also has a constantly updated collection of magazines and journals on Japanese culture, some of which are complete as far back as the 1930s. The photographs on the walls depict some of the key moments in the life of Maraini, who was also a Himalayan mountain-climber. Not only are there pictures of the historic expeditions by the great Orientalist Giuseppe Tucci (in 1937 and 1948) and of expeditions by the Italian Alpine Club to Karakorum and the Hindu Kush region, but images of a range of countries in the Far East and South-East Asia: from Japan to Pakistan, Nepal to Tibet, Korea to Cambodia. Such a series of fascinating journeys and adventures reflects the boundless curiosity that inspired Fosco Maraini throughout his life.

If the writer wished to bequeath his precious library and photographic archive to the Gabinetto Vieusseux, he was in part inspired by a desire to re-establish the connection between the continent he loved and the city of his birth, for up to the 1930s there had been close scientific links between Florence and Asia.

What is striking is the breadth and homogeneity of this collection dedicated to Asia, the multiple aspects of the continent being illustrated by both texts and images. The photographic archive by itself is remarkable and would be the pride of even the most selective of universities.

There are other fascinating rooms in the Gabinetto Vieusseux, but the Sala Maraini is unique in Florence. The staff are welcoming and the director himself is very helpful. Wandering amidst these books and images, you can – within the very heart of Piazza Strozzi – engage in a voyage of rediscovery that takes you back over the highlights of a long-running "love affair" between a Florentine and the Far East.

SCULPTURE OF A LITTLE DEVIL ⑭

A devil on a horse

On the corner of Palazzo Vecchietti at the junction of Via degli Strozzi and Via de' Vecchietti is a bronze statue of an insolent, jeering little devil. The work of Giambologna (or Jean de Boulogne,

Douai, 1529 – Florence, 1608), it was commissioned by Bernardo Vecchietti to commemorate a mysterious incident in Florence's history.

In 1425 a Dominican friar, Pietro da Verona (see below), a sort of precursor of Savonarola, was preaching against heresy in Piazza del Mercato Vecchio (now Piazza della Repubblica) when a startled black horse ran into the square. The monk, immediately realising that this was a ruse of the Devil to distract his listeners, raised his hand to make a large sign of the cross over the satanic beast.

The possessed beast withdrew and disappeared around the corner of Palazzo Vecchietti, leaving nothing but a plume of smoke and a strong smell of sulphur.

Pietro da Verona

Pietro da Verona, or St Peter Martyr, was born in Verona in 1205 to a Cathar family. Having become a Dominican, he gained a reputation for his visceral opposition to heretical ideas and was appointed head inquisitor for Lombardy, where he became known for the number of victims he condemned to burn at the stake. When he later moved to Florence, he established a sort of Christian militia to fight against the Patarini, a movement of clergy and populace rebelling against the excesses of certain prelates and their way of life. It is said that he feared his life would come to violent end due to the hatred he aroused. And that is what happened on April 6 1252, when a certain Pietro da Balsamo split his head open with a billhook; the murderer later repented his crime and himself became a Dominican. In the numerous paintings of this murder, one sees the saint almost impervious to the cleaver buried in his skull. Only two years after his death, he was canonised as St Peter Martyr by Pope Innocent IV, who thus exalted the role he had played in fighting heresy. Two violent clashes are said to have occurred in 1244. Historians now have cast doubts on such stories, even if there are two columns in Florence that were raised to commemorate these events: one, la Colonna della Croce al Trebbio, stands at the corner of Via del Moro, Via delle Belle Donne and Via del Trebbio, the other, la colonna Santa Felicità, stands in the square of the same name.

TRACES OF THE INTERIOR OF THE PALAZZO DELLA LANA

Fourtheenth-century frescoes and high vaults ....

Via Calimala, 14r, 16r, 22r

The ground floor of the Palazzo dell'Arte della Lana (the Wool Guild, one of the seven Florentine arts and crafts guilds), in Via Calimala, is now occupied by a row of three shops well worth a visit as they still have their original interiors.

At number 16r, the frescoes depict some of the stages in wool processing, all the more interesting because few such contemporary views exist.

At 22r, a small chapel is dedicated to the fifteenth-century Italian painter known as Master of the Bargello. On the whole, the rooms have been tastefully restored, in line with detailed conservation restrictions. An effort has even been made to reinstate much of the original colour to the frescoes, although sometimes the touching-up has been rather carelessly done.

At 14r, large blocks of exposed stonework form an entire wall that was part of the street in the Middle Ages, then became the inner wall of a palazzo extension before its current incarnation.

NEARBY

Column of Abundance: a persecuted statue   ⑯

It was difficult to pay tribute to the Roman Goddess of Abundance in Florence, because the ancient statue on a column in the city centre, on the present site of Piazza della Repubblica, had been lost. In 1431 it was replaced with Donatello's *Dovizia* (Abundance), complete with a bell to signal the opening and closing of the Mercato Vecchio, and another bell at the end of a chain to which dishonest merchants were attached. But this statue, destroyed in 1721 by subsidence, was in its turn replaced with a work by Giovan Battista Foggini. The column was hidden by part of the market buildings, leaving only the statue visible above roof level. This column and its statue were later dismantled and the sections dispersed. Then in 1956 a copy of Foggini's statue was erected on a new column in Piazza della Repubblica, where it still stands today, marking the point where three districts converge: Santa Maria Novella, San Giovanni and Santa Croce – the true heart of Florence.

PICTURE OF THE DESECRATOR

Sixteenth-century cartoon strip depicting the punishment for desecration

Santa Maria de' Ricci church • Via del Corso, 25
Open from 10.30am to 8pm • The church is sometimes closed at lunchtime
Curate's telephone: 333 3074339

Almost opposite the entrance to Vicolo del Panico, the church of Santa Maria de' Ricci contains (at the far end of the last chapel on the left) a reproduction of a painting that is divided into nine framed scenes, rather like an early cartoon strip. These images recount how the church was built and dedicated to the Virgin as an act of reparation for the sacrilege that had been committed on July 21 1501.

On the evening of that day, Antonio di Giovanni Rinaldeschi was passing by, having lost all his money at dice in the Albergo del Fico (Fig Inn). Happening to walk near a niche with an image of the Annunciation, he vented his anger by picking up a lump of horse dung and hurling it in the Virgin's face, an act of sacrilege that shocked all those present. Although partly due to excessive drinking, this outburst of anger cost Rinaldeschi his life: he was arrested, taken to the Bagello prison, given a summary trial and then hung from one of the building's windows.

The image of the Annunciation that was the object of this sacrilege is now in the choir of Santa Maria de' Ricci church, and the last chapel on the left has a reproduction of the cartoon strip telling the whole story. Better still, go to the Museo Stibbert, where you can see the sixteenth-century original, which has recently been restored.

For those interested to learn more, there is William J. Connell and Giles Constable's *Sacrilege and Redemption in Renaissance Florence: The Case of Antonio Rinaldeschi*, published in 2005. When an incident becomes a cartoon strip, it enjoys a certain popular success. Other narratives "crystallise" around it, revealing popular attitudes and beliefs.

ANTICO VICOLO DEL PANICO OR VICOLO DELLO SCANDALO

The alleyway that was opened up to separate the homes of two rival families

From the Corso to Via Dante Alighieri

Of all the alleyways that cut through the heart of the old city centre there is one that does not appear on any map. This is the narrow Vicolo del Panico, whose name has nothing to do with "panic" – the accent is on the second syllable – but rather refers to a type of grain. To make things even more confusing, there is also another, official, Vicolo del Panico, which does appear on maps: it is a dead end leading off Via Pellicceria. To find the "unofficial" alleyway, you have to go to No.49r in the Corso, where an opening leads through to 8 Via Dante Alighieri (where, it would seem, the poet's house once stood). Spanned at intervals by arches, this narrow twisting alleyway has a story that is even stranger than its name. It dates from the Middle Ages, when violent internal fighting was common in Florence. Following the victory of the Guelphs over the Ghibellines, the victors themselves were split by a schism between the Cerchi family and the more populist "White Guelphs" and the Domati family and the "Black Guelphs" who represented the more affluent classes. Certain families within a specific district thus found themselves living near – or right next-door to – their new enemies. And it was very easy for someone to slip through a dividing wall in order to attack, rob or simply torment members of the opposing faction; some even feared that the dividing walls might be totally demolished to make way for a full-scale assault. This is why the city authorities decided that the dividing walls of such houses should be knocked down and replaced by a narrow alleyway separating "enemy" homes. One such alley was Vicolo del Panico, which was soon passing by the popular name of Vicolo dello Scandalo.

This alley remains one of the rare examples of such "peacekeeping" within the very fabric of the old city centre. The other Vicolo del Panico was named in the nineteenth century, when obviously the reasons behind the creation of the first no longer existed.

Zabaione: invented by St Pasquale Baylon to restore flagging masculine fervour

Santa Margherita is also where the Confraternity of Chefs used to gather. Their patron saint, St Pasquale Baylon, deserves his position because he is said to have invented the recipe for zabaione:

1 egg yolk + 2 glasses of marsala + 2 spoonfuls of sugar + 1 glass of water.

He devised the recipe not in his spare time in the kitchen but as part of his pastoral activities. It was prescribed for those women who complained their husbands were no longer "up to the job".

THE FIRST CERTIFIED PORTRAIT OF DANTE

A rare gem

Palazzo dell'Arte dei Giudici e dei Notai
Via del Proconsolo, 16r
Open daily from 9am to 5pm
For reservation: telephone 055 240618 or e-mail museo@artenotai.org
www.artenotai.org
Admission: €8

The premises of the old Guild of Judges and Notaries were restored in 2005, offering the opportunity not only for archaeological excavations in the basement but also for the creation of a restaurant on the ground floor and a museum on the first floor. It is the latter which contains a rare gem: the first certified portraits of Dante and Boccaccio. It was during the restoration of the frescoed walls of the first floor that various discoveries were made: the so-called Sant'Ivo lunette, a lunette of the *Arti del Trivio letterario* [depicting the figures of Grammar, Rhetoric and Dialectics] and a lunette with the portraits of the four writers who were considered to be the "founding fathers" of the Florentine Republic – at least, of the Republic as envisaged by Coluccio Salutati, the chancellor of Palazzo Vecchio. The portraits of two of these figures (Petrarch and Zanobi da Strada) have all but disappeared, with the exception of a few fragments. However, at either end of the composition you can clearly identify Dante and Boccaccio. Critics have no doubt about the authenticity of the Dante portrait, which shows a face which corresponds to the one depicted in the nearby Cappella della Maddalena frescoes in the Bargello (painted 1336-1337): the skin is slightly dark and the nose has its famous aquiline form, even if it is not hooked. Over the period of a century, famous artists painted other portraits here, with the palazzo becoming a veritable workshop for the city's homage to the literature in which it took such pride: Andrea del Castagno painted Leonardo Bruni, Ambrogio di Baldese painted Coluccio Salutati and the Latin poet Claudian (believed to be a native of Florence), and Pollaiolo painted Poggio Bracciolini.

NEARBY

Traces of a medieval tower ㉑

Still in Via del Proconsolo, just before you reach the Alle Murate restaurant, two concentric bands of copper on the pavement mark the circumference of a medieval tower.

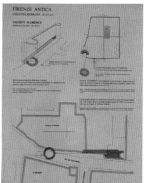

Dante, the Templars and I Fedeli d'Amore

The age of Dante Alighieri (1265-1321) was profoundly marked by the decline of the Order of the Knights Templars, and above all by the series of persecutions, imprisonments and condemnations to which the Order was subjected following its interdiction by the king of France, Philip IV, and Pope Clement V (clearly manipulated by the former). These events had a powerful impact upon Dante, who denounced this injustice before the political powers of the day. He went so far as to take part in an event in Florence that was a deliberate expression of support for Pope Boniface VIII, who in 1302 had been denounced as a heretic by the *États Généraux* summoned by Philip IV; in 1303, the king sent his troops to Florence to hold the pontiff prisoner in Palazzo d'Agnani for three days. The Templars, who were the pope's personal guard, were on this occasion supported by the local burghers, including Dante, and managed to free Pope Boniface VIII. However, he died just a month later in rather unclear circumstances; some even mentioned poison. Philip IV supported the immediate election of Clement V and set about persecuting the Templars, ultimately procuring their total destruction – in spite of the fact that a delegation (of which Dante was a part) had gone to Rome to argue their case before the pope in 1307. It is thought that Dante's initiation into the social and religious ideals underpinning the Templars came when he frequented their Florentine headquarters at San Jacopo, in Campo Corbolini. In this area, the Templars are credited with the original construction of the church of San Jacopo Sopr'Arno. The Order aimed to promote, within the Christian faith and thence society as a whole, their ideal of spiritual perfection and temporal justice. To this end, they used poetry, song and the prose works of the Confraternity of Troubadours, advocates of a philosophy of "spiritual love" who were continually at loggerheads with the dominion exerted by Rome. Dante himself was one of these *Fedeli d'Amore* [The Faithful of Love]. The Confraternity of troubadours and minstrels had spread throughout the whole of Europe. The first traces of it are to be found in the poetry of the tenth and eleventh centuries, in courtly praise to the Mother of God and celebrations of the blessings of humanity. In a sense the descendants of the ancient *vates* (soothsayers) and bards, the troubadours wrote under the guidance of important spiritual masters, producing love songs and satirical lyrics that expressed esoteric truths. In short, they might be described as the "mouthpiece" of the different esoteric Orders that then existed in Europe, and there was a profound relation between their poetry and the kind of spirituality championed by the Templars. Disgusted by the bloody destruction of the Order of the Knights Templars, Dante wanted to set the record straight for future generations, giving a masterly explication of its true aims in his literary masterpiece *La Divina Commedia*. It is interesting, for example, that in his *Paradiso*, from the third heaven inwards the poet is guided through the heavens towards his vision of God by St Bernard of Clairvaux, who had been the spiritual father of the Templars. Similarly, when he reaches the highest of the heavens, the poet rediscovers Beatrice, his beloved and the expression of divine grace. There he has a vision of a white rose with a triangle at its centre; the latter symbolises love of the Holy Trinity, whilst the rose itself had been a symbol adopted by the *Fedeli d'Amore*. The very decision to write the poem in the vernacular – the local dialect of *Toscan*, which is very close to modern-day Italian – was a gesture of revolt against Rome and its ecclesiastical Latin. It is also significant that in the eighth circle of hell called *Malebolge* (Fraud), Dante places two popes: Boniface VIII, condemned for simony (the sale of ecclesiastical honours) and Clement V, the corrupt pope who signed the condemnation of the Templars. A "comedy" not because it is comic but because it ends well for all the characters who gain admission to Heaven, *La Divina Commedia* is made up of 100 canti and a total of 14,233 lines. Its three parts (*Paradiso*, *Purgatorio* and *Inferno*) are each made up of 33 canti of 40 to 50 tercets (verses of three lines). The *Inferno* also has an introductory canto, thus bringing the total of *canti* to 100; a symbol of absolute perfection ($100=10\times10$ = the perfection of that which is perfect), this number is also to be found, for example, in the 100 names of the God of Islam. Each *canto* is made up of 130 to 140 lines of *terza rima* (that is, interlocking tercets). Thus, you continually find multiples of the numbers 3, 7 and 10, all of which were heavily symbolic in the Middle Ages and might be taken to express the poet's devotion to the Holy Trinity, a special object of devotion for the Templars themselves. *Terza rima* here involves hendecasyllabic lines (11 syllables) organised in rhymes that follow the schema ABA, BCB, CDC, EDE, and so on, with the central line of one tercet rhyming with the first and third of the following one. This structure is also known as "Dante's tercet", because he was the first to use it. Furthermore, the three books of the *Commedia* all end in a rhyme on the same word: Stelle (stars). It should be remembered that Mary, the mother of Christ, was often referred to as *Stella Maris* and again was an object of particular devotion for the Templars.

Beatrice: the Path of Spiritual Enlightenment

 Dante says he met Beatrice when he was 18 years old, even if he had first noticed her when he was nine and she eight. Some argue that he only saw her once and that he never even spoke to her. There is no biographical evidence to prove the matter one way or another. Solely on the basis of the biographical information that Dante himself supplies in *La Vita Nuova*, we know that Beatrice (Bice) Portinari was born in 1265/66 and died on June 8 1290. She has been identified as the daughter of the banker Folco Portinari from Portico di Romagna, who left her a substantial sum of money in his will dated 1287. We also know that Beatrice married the Florentine nobleman Simone de Bardi, by whom she had six daughters, and lived in a house next to Dante's in Florence. She founded the Ospedale di Santa Maria Nuova, today the hospital of central Florence. Dante's dithyrambic praise of her Christian charity has immortalised her as *Beata Beatrice* [Blessed Beatrice]; it was under this name that Dante Gabriel Rossetti painted her in 1864, in a picture which shows the dove of the Holy Spirit appearing to her whilst carrying a rose in its beak. The rose was the symbol of the *Fidelli d'Amore* (see p. 48) and also the flower of spiritual enlightenment and revelation. This is why the Litany of the Blessed Virgin Mary mentions a "mystic rose".

The courtly love of the twelfth and thirteenth centuries – for the first time since the Gnostics of the second and third centuries – glorified the spiritual dignity and religious virtue of women. Gnostic texts, for example, had exulted the Mother of God at the same time as the "mystical silence" of the Holy Spirit and the Wisdom of God. If medieval devotions to the Virgin were an indirect veneration of women, Dante went one step further: he deified Beatrice, proclaiming her as superior to the angels and saints, as invulnerable to sin and almost comparable to the Virgin herself. Thus, when Beatrice is about to appear within the Earthly Paradise, a voice proclaims: "Come, O my spouse, from Lebanon" (*Purgatorio*, XXX, 11) – a famous line from the *Song of Songs* (IV, 8) which had been used by the Church in its veneration of the Mother of God. In another passage (*Purgatorio*, XXXIII, 10), Beatrice applies to herself words that had first been used by Christ: "A little while, and ye shall not see me; and again, a little while, and ye shall see me." (John 16.16) Beatrice represents Wisdom and thus the mystery of Salvation; Dante introduces her during the course of his three journeys of initiation into Hell, Purgatory and Heaven. She is presented as the idealisation of the Eternal Woman, the chosen means of communication that can lead to the metaphysical re-awakening and salvation of humankind. This view of love and the veneration of womanhood as playing a part in the salvation of the human soul inspired the gnosis and esoteric initiations of the *Fidelli d'Amore* – as you can see in *La Vita Nuova* [New Life], which Dante dedicates to Beatrice. Written in 1292/93, this work describes initiation through spiritual love, with the figure of Woman being a symbol of *Intellectus illuminatio*, of the transcendent Spirit and Divine Wisdom that are destined to awaken the Christian world from the lethargy to which it has succumbed as a result of the spiritual ignobility of the popes. Thus, in the medieval writings of the *Fidelli d'Amore* they are allusions to "a widow who is not such". This was the *Madonna Intelligenza*, who had become a "widow" because her spouse – the pope – was dead to the spiritual, having given himself over entirely to temporal affairs and corruption. The veneration of the "Unique Woman" – and initiation into the mysteries of Love – were part of what made the *Fidelli d'Amore* into a sort of secret spiritual militia, employing an encoded language for truths that were to remain concealed from "the vulgar". This need for secrecy was urged by one of the most famous *Fidelli*, Francesco de Barberino (1264-1348), whilst another, Jacques de Baisieux, would say: "one must not reveal the counsels of love, but rather keep them carefully hidden". Scattered throughout Europe, the *Fidelli d'Amore* were linked with the troubadours and minstrels of the day, exalting the ideal of the Eternal Woman as associated with the supreme gift of the Holy Spirit (to which they referred as "Holy Love"). The veneration of Our Lady was their way of asserting the presence of the Paraclete (or "comforter") amongst the people with whom they settled. Royal courts were readily open to the *Fidelli*, themselves becoming "courts of love": this was famously true of the court of Alfonso X the Wise, King of Leon and Castille, and the court of Dinis I, the "troubadour" King of Portugal.

The *Fidelli* was not a heretical movement, but rather a group of free-thinking writers and artists who opposed the corruption of the Church and no longer recognised the popes as the spiritual head of Christendom. This opposition became keener after the bloody extermination of the Order of the Knights Templars by the King of France, Philip IV, and his "agent", Pope Clement V. So, setting aside actual biographical details, the Beatrice of Dante's poem is, above all, a symbol of the Perfect Woman, of Divine Grace, and of the amorous soul that is a guarantee of spiritual immortality. Exemplifying the path of mystical purification, Beatrice represents that inner awakening which took place in Dante after his period of exile and his peregrinations in search of purification – peregrinations that finally came to an end when he rediscovered his immortal soul, symbolised by Beatrice.

"GIUSEPPE GARIBALDI" VETERANS' ㉑ AND OLD SOLDIERS' MUSEUM

Old Garibaldi Tower

Torre della Castagna
Piazza San Martino, 1
Tel: 055 2396104
Open Thursday afternoon from 4pm to 6pm

This museum is not devoted solely to Garibaldi but to the "veterans and old soldiers" who played a part in the great epic of Garibaldi and his "Redshirts". Of course, all that took place 150 years ago and the veterans are long gone, so the existence of such a museum may seem an extravaganza due solely to a local association of enthusiasts. In fact, this association is spread nationwide in twenty-seven different branches, which bring together not only those with a passion for the period of the Risorgimento but also the old partisans of Garibaldi Division who fought in the former Yugoslavia. In Florence, the association owns a little gem, for its premises occupy the ground floor, mezzanine and first floor of one of the finest medieval towers in the city, Torre della Castagna. This tower, originally called Torre Baccadiferro, was renamed when the Florentine priors moved here in the thirteenth century. They had at first lived in the Bargello district but – as the passage from Dino Compagni's *Chronicles* cited on the nearby wall plaque records – they then took the decision "to shut themselves away within the Castagna Tower in order to put an end to threats from the powerful". This tower was indeed a small fortress, particularly robust because – unlike most of the other towers in Florence – it had not been modified or damaged, and it is now one of the few towers open to the public. The credit for this is due to the Garibaldi Association, which readily opens its doors to all those who wish to consult its library of works relating not only to Garibaldi (obviously enough) but also the Renaissance. Once a week (on Thursday) you can also visit the curious museum that has been laid out within its small rooms: the collection comprises Garibaldi memorabilia, swords, other weapons, medals, portraits, busts … and the famous cushion used by the general. In short, not only an insight into a specific period of history but also the chance to see the inside of this superb tower.

Origin of the term "ballot"

In Florence, the chestnuts (*castagne*) which the Florentine priors used when casting their votes are still called *ballotte*. Perhaps this is the origin of the verb "to ballot".

PALAZZO UGUCCIONI

A non-aligned palazzo

Piazza della Signoria, 7
Open on the first working Monday of the month from 9am to 12 noon and 3pm to 6pm, visits by appointment at 055 4934497

As if wishing to draw attention to itself, Palazzo Uguccioni juts out into Piazza della Signoria, out of line with the adjacent buildings. This was done according to the wishes of Giovanni Uguccioni, who began construction in 1550 after obtaining Grand Duke Cosimo I's permission to build his palazzo there. The neighbours objected to modifications to the "row" of buildings on this side of the piazza, which delayed the project somewhat, but the grand duke once again intervened to bring it to a successful conclusion.

This was no minor privilege, for the Uguccioni palazzo stands opposite Palazzo Vecchio, and such an exemption from basic urban planning implied a privileged relationship with the court.

Besides, Cosimo had every interest in improving the appearance of the city's seat of power, and the Uguccioni made sure that their palazzo was smaller, as if to say that their aspirations were still subject to the regulations.

However, it was built in a much more monumental and sophisticated style than the palazzi next door, with three arches and *pietra forte* (sandstone) rustication on the ground floor and double columns on the upper floors, their pedestals carved with the family coat of arms.

The care taken on the façade is not replicated in the interior, however, which incorporated rooms from the pre-existing buildings, although they do have some valuable frescoes. It may be small, but this palazzo is patently the work of an exhibitionist. Giovanni Uguccioni might even have built it in the centre of the piazza had he been allowed to do so.

NEARBY

An authentic medieval palazzo (23)

Palazzo dei Cerchi
Vicolo dei Cerchi, 1
Open first Friday of the month from 10am to 1pm by appointment
Tel: 055 294926

For those wishing to visit a real medieval building in Florence, the Palazzo dei Cerchi is one of the best preserved. The palazzo, which is built on a vertical plan, incorporates several converted tower houses and is faced with exposed stonework, including one of the oldest examples of rustication in Florence. Once past the pointed arches of the entrance, you enter frescoed halls and climb up through wooden-panelled rooms with vaulted ceilings, to the last room at the top of the tower, to find yourself in the historical and geographical heart of Florence.

Another Florentine invention: ice cream

Florence saw the invention not only of visual perspective (Leon Battista Alberti), Italian literature (Dante) and the telephone (Antonio Meucci), but also of ice cream. Such a delicious dessert could only be the brainchild of an artist, indeed, of a scholar-artist: Bernardo Buontalenti (1531–1608). In fact, this engineer, architect, decorator and inventor perfected previous attempts to create such a dish: before him, another Florentine by the name of Ruggeri had produced a sorbet for a cookery competition, which was described as "the most unusual dish that has ever existed". It was for the official visit of the Spanish to Florence that the grand duke ordered Buontalenti to come up with a dessert that would "leave these foreigners – in particular, these Spaniards – gawping". So the engineer invented ice cream – or, more exactly, a mix of milk and egg yolk blended together with honey as a sweetener, a drop of wine to heighten the taste and a pinch of salt to lower the freezing point. This was no longer sorbet, made by mixing snow and fruit, but rather real ice cream with a smooth, milky texture. Of course, the history of ice cream did not stop there. Various improvements followed – for example, those introduced by Procope, a Sicilian chef working in Paris. However, the success of Florentine ice cream was such that Florence – and nowhere else – still produces the famous, smooth "Buontalenti" ice cream. In 1979, the ice cream shop Badiani (Viale dei Mille, 20r) won the prize for the best "Buontalenti" in Florence – a very special flavour that is still protected by copyright. Other excellent ice-cream makers have also produced their own variety – including Baroncini (an old dairy business that has since 1946 been located at Via Celso, 3r) and Da Roberto (Via Mariti, 3r). The number of historic ice cream shops in the city bears witness to

BUONTALENTI

the importance of this business in Florence over the centuries. These include the Gelateria Alpina (open since 1929 at Viale Strozzi, 12r) and Gelateria Veneta (open since 1925 at Piazza Beccaria, 7r). The Gelateria Vivoli (open since 1930 at Via Isola delle Stinche, 7r) is special because here you can not only enjoy the place's famous ice cream but also find a buchetta on the outside wall and, inside, a room decorated with a fresco of the Ponte Vecchio by Luigi Falai, a pupil of Piero Annigoni.

THE FRESCOES
IN *ANTICO RISTORANTE PAOLI*

㉔

An old trattoria where Boccaccio meets Art Nouveau

Via dei Tavolini, 12r
Tel: 055 216215

Boccaccio plays a leading role in the decor of the Antico Ristorante Paoli. Opened as a *trattoria-salumeria* by Pietro Paoli in 1824, this place with its typical marble tables is decorated with various works of art. Amongst them note the three lunettes frescoed with scenes from Boccaccio's *Decameron*. They were painted by Carlo Coppede, who in 1916 was commissioned to decorate the restaurant – thus perpetuating a tradition which had seen various artists work here at different periods in its history. The small *Saletta delle Rose* [Rose Room], for example, has splendid painted and ceramic decoration by one of the most important exponents of Italian Art Nouveau, Galileo Chini, who worked here just a few years later. The Villa Pecori Giraldi Museum in Borgo San Lorenzo is dedicated entirely to the work of this artist, one of whose descendants, Antonio Chini, decorated the Cantina Guidi.

The trattoria's collection contains other works, including a bust of the American president Woodrow Wilson, a painting by Annigoni (who also has his own museum in Florence; see p. 284), ceramics by Cantagalli dedicated to the various communes of Tuscany, and other valuable paintings.

BAS-RELIEF OF THE LOST HOOF

The incident behind the church building

Bas-relief of the lost hoof
Church of Orsanmichele
Via Arte della Lana, 9
Open from 10am to 5pm (closed Monday)

To the right of the rear door of Orsanmichele, a small bas-relief illustrates the decisive incident thought to have led to the construction of this church in the eighth century. The scene represented by Nanni di Banco, also responsible for some of the statues outside the building, is curious to say the least and has nothing biblical or noble about it. It concerns a farrier, a horse and the horse's lost hoof, which magically reattached itself.

This bas-relief is the symbolic synthesis of a complicated story. After his death, the young and diligent St Michael appeared several times in his father's dreams, asking him to build a chapel in the fields beside their house. In the meantime, without any explanation, someone secretly began to replenish the hay in the barn and clean out the horses during the night. Until the day that one of the horses lost a shoe … and when the farrier arrived the entire hoof dropped off, to the alarm of bystanders. But, as if by some wondrous act, the hoof reattached itself to the horse's leg. After such a miracle, it didn't take long to build the church of "Orsanmichele". The name derives from "San Michele negli orti" (Kitchen

Garden of St Michael) because, at the time, the site was known for its kitchen gardens.

The first church was later replaced by the Arnolfo di Cambio grain market, which was converted into the present building. The layout of the covered market, with its unusual parallelepiped shape, the two interior aisles and even a pillar that served as a kind of grain store, has been preserved. A long rectangular crevice can still be seen from which the grain was poured down a stone chute.

NEARBY

Assembly Hall of the Accademia delle Arti del Disegno ㉖

Via Orsanmichele, 4 • Tel: 055 219642 – www.aadfi.it
Open during secretariat hours and the frequent conferences

Just a stone's throw from Orsanmichele, the Palazzo dell'Arte dei Beccai houses the Academy of Art and Design, one of the oldest academies in the world (it was founded over 450 years ago by Cosimo I, at the suggestion of Giorgio Vasari, in 1563). There is a small gallery with portraits of past presidents, as well as works by old masters such as Mariotto di Nardo's Florentine Gothic *Madonna with Saints* and Jacopo Pontormo's *Tabernacle of Boldrone*. You can also see the mysterious *Virgin with Book*, attributed to Pontormo, although two books are in the painting: the Virgin holds one open in her right hand while the other is in the arms of an enigmatic figure standing in the background to the right.

27

FRESCO OF ST ANNE

St Anne, Florence's forgotten patron saint

Church of Orsanmichele
Via dell'Arte della Lana, 9
Ground floor open Tuesday–Sunday from 10am to 5pm; closed Monday.
The sculpture museum (first floor) open Monday only from 10am to 5pm;
Admission free

Among its various treasures, the church of Orsanmichele has a painting unique of its kind. On the curtain wall of the oratory, Mariotto di Nardo painted a fresco in the late fourteenth century that depicts St Anne in a rather curious posture: she is shown holding the city of Florence in her arms. Most saints are depicted at the moment of martyrdom or being venerated, but it is much rarer to see one clasping an entire city to her breast. The iconography denotes a very special relationship between saint and city. If you ask any Florentine, they will tell you without hesitation that the patron saint of the city is St John the Baptist, whose feast day (24 June) is celebrated with the famous "St John Fireworks". But everyone seems to have forgotten that Florence has another patron saint: St Anne, who is depicted here within a building that symbolises both the spiritual and physical well-being of the city (Orsanmichele served as a granary as well as a church). It was for this building that the city authorities commissioned a statue of St Anne from Francesco di Sangallo in 1522, to stand near the altar dedicated to her. For centuries, St Anne's feast day (July 26) was celebrated in great pomp as an expression of the freedoms enjoyed by the Florentines. The saint was then adopted by the de' Medici as the patron of their dynasty. However, with the advent of the Counter-Reformation emphasis shifted onto Anne's role as the mother of the Virgin Mary, and it is only fairly recently that the city authorities have re-established the celebration of July 26, which involves – among other events – a procession in front of Orsanmichele. These festivities are still quite a subdued affair compared with the fireworks that celebrate St John the Baptist – to whom various churches are dedicated (including Giovanni Michelucci's "motorway church") and a number of historic confraternities and guilds. Still, St Anne does have a unique privilege: she is the one shown embracing the city of Florence.

Why was St Anne chosen as the patron saint of Florence?

It was on July 26 1343 – St Anne's feast day – that Florence threw off the "foreign" rule exercised by Walter VI, Count of Brienne and Duke of Athens. Hence, the association of the saint with the city's freedoms.

THE STRONGBOX
IN THE NAPAPIJRI SHOP

28

The merchants' strongbox

Via Porta Rossa, 2r, on the corner of Via Calimaruzza
Ask the staff, they will accompany you

Napapijri, a sportswear shop in Via Porta Rossa, contains a largely-unknown treasure: a magnificent strongbox fitted within the dividing wall. According to experts, this masterpiece of craftsmanship dates from the fifteenth or sixtheenth century – only in a city like Florence could such an antique crop up in such an unlikely place. In effect, the strongbox is a combination of marvels: within the stone wall a small niche was hollowed, within which was set a small nail-studded wooden door. However, this was only the first wall of defence in the strongbox, a veritable masterpiece of the locksmith's art (all the keys are original). Curiously, the receptacle in which precious objects were placed is not made of metal or wood; it is formed from sheets of sandstone fitted into the wall. Thus, at least three different materials – stone, metal and wood – were required to make this strongbox. In the same shop there are also several capitals engraved with eagles clasping a bale of fabric (*torsello*) in their claws. They indicate that this was one of the halls of the *Arte di Calimala*, a rich guild involved in money-changing and the wool trade in medieval Florence. So the strongbox was likely created to hold precious documents or property of the guild or one of its members. Founded in 1182 by textile merchants, the *Arte di Calimala* played an im-

portant role in the history of the wool and textile trades. However, in 1770 it was closed by order of Grand Duke Piero Leopoldo I, when all the old guilds and corporations were replaced by a new Chamber of Commerce.

The origin of the name Calimala

The etymology of this curious term is unclear. Some say it comes from the *Calle Maia* [Main Street] of Roman times, whilst others argue that it is derived from *callis malus* [street of ill-repute]. There are even some who argue it is derived from the Greek *kalos mallos* [fine wool]. Note that the street sign identifies this not as *Via di Calimala* but simply as *Calimala*.

SCALES AT THE FARMACIA DEL CINGHIALE

Comfortable balance

Piazza del Mercato Nuovo, 4r
Tel: 055 214221
Open from 9am to 1pm and 3.30pm to 8pm

The statue of the boar (*cinghiale*) gives its name not only to Loggia del Porcellino but also to another historic pharmacy within Florence, in Piazza del Mercato Nuovo. It was here that, in 1752, Girolamo Niccolò Branchi della Torre, an enlightened spirit of the day, would for a select audience of scholars and enthusiasts perform a series of chemical experiments that reflected the gradual shift from alchemy to the modern science of chemistry; indeed, the grand duke would call upon Branchi della Torre when setting up Tuscany's first rigorously scientific school of chemistry. The pharmacy, frequented by artists and men of letters, developed a sophisticated range of body products: creams, perfumes, oils and essences – all made with natural ingredients and all still available today. Unfortunately, the premises of this historic pharmacy were badly damaged by the disastrous flood of 1966, although various precious furnishings did survive and are worth going out of your way to see. One of them is particularly interesting: an amazing pair of scales that lets you weigh yourself while seated comfortably in a specially designed chair. Based on the sort of scales the Romans used for weighing people, this is an apparatus that "indulges" the lazy and the overweight.

CEILING OF THE PALAGIO DI PARTE GUELFA LIBRARY ARCHIVE

A little-known wonder

Piazzetta di Parte Guelfa
Open Monday–Friday from 9am to 10pm and Saturday 9am to 1pm,
Monday from 9am to 2pm for consultation only
Tel: 055 2616029 / 2616030
bibliotecapalagio@comune.fi.it
www.biblioteche.comune.fi.it/biblioteca_palagio_di_parte_guelfa/

The 35,000-volume heritage of Palagio di Parte Guelfa library is housed in a deconsecrated church, Santa Maria di San Biagio.

It has two rooms: the reading room and the superb periodicals archive in the old chapel of San Bartolomeo, which was built in 1345 at the initiative of Canon Federigo di Bartolo Bardi.

Although incomplete, the decorations and scenes of this hall, attributed to the Giotto school, are magnificent.

On the ceiling, against a backdrop of elegant golden lilies on a field of azure (a motif found around the city in memory of its ancestral link with the reigning house of France and in particular with Saint Louis), the emblems of the crafts guilds (*arti*) surround the emblem of Guelph Florence, with the pope's coat of arms in the centre.

The name of the library comes from the neighbouring Palagio di Parte Guelfa, the former palace (*palagio*) and seat of the political faction of the Guelphs in the thirteenth century. The building was enlarged over the following centuries, apparently a project of Brunelleschi, and today it is the centre of the *calcio storico* (an early form of football) and the Florentine Republic's historical costume parade, as well as an exhibition space.

Dating back to 1308, the church of Santa Maria di San Biagio owes its name to the fact that it stood near the Santa Maria gate, one of the entrances to the city in the Carolingian ramparts (ninth century AD). The church was then modified as a meeting-place for the captains of the Guelph faction. Faithful to the papacy, by the end of the thirteenth century the Guelphs had taken over the city to the detriment of the Ghibellines, who were sympathetic to the Holy Roman emperors.

When the palace was built, the church lost its role of meeting-place while retaining its purely religious status. In the fifteenth century it was dedicated to St Blaise (San Biagio). It was subsequently deconsecrated to become, at first, a storage depot for the ceremonial carts for the Palio horse race and the fireworks intended for the traditional Scoppio del Carro (Explosion of the Cart) Easter ritual; and then, from 1785, the Florentine fire station.

In 1944, it was also the home of Gabinetto Vieusseux, one of Florence's oldest and best-known scientific-literary cultural institutions.

Souvenir of the medieval Florentine Carroccio

Loggia del Porcellino, Piazza del Mercato Nuovo

At the centre of the Loggia del Porcellino take note of a curious detail, which may be missed among all the market stalls; to get a good look, it's better to get there before 11am or after 8pm, when the area is clear. On the floor is an engraving in marble of a six-spoked wheel, which commemorates the site where the Florentine *Carroccio* stood: this was a large four-wheeled chariot adorned with the city's coat of arms, around which medieval soldiers would gather when going into battle. The wheel was also used to punish insolvent debtors, guilty of a crime that was unpardonable in such a mercantile city as Florence. The punishment, repeated three times, involved the debtor being forced down abruptly, hitting his backside (culo) on the wheel. This practice was at the roots of various local expressions: scu-

lo (bad luck) and *restare col culo per terra* ("to be broke"; literally, "be left with your backside on the ground"). Finally, note the small door in one of the corner columns. This leads to a narrow staircase that takes you up to a loft under the roof of the loggia. Unnoticeable from outside, this vast hall is used nowadays for occasional meetings or private dinner parties.

Traditional ritual involving the famous Porcellino

Tourists seem to have taken the famous Porcellino to their hearts as much as the Florentines have. Tradition demands that once you get here you have to perform the following actions: 1) point out that the name of porcellino (piglet) is rather unsuitable as this is a full-grown boar; 2) rub the animal's snout, as have millions before you (judging by its high polish); 3) make a wish; 4) put a coin in the statue's mouth; 5) let it drop into the fountain; 6) note whether it catches on the grating or falls through; only the latter brings good luck, so in the former case start again. This is an odd type of "sacrifice" to a statue which is less a celebration of the wild boar than of the artistic copy: the present statue is a copy of a work by the seventeenth-century sculptor Pietro Tacca, which is now in the Pitti Palace, and that original itself was inspired by a Greek statue in the Uffizi.

PLAQUE TO GIUSEPPE LACHERI ㉜

Celebrating a market trader

Piazza del Mercato Nuovo, corner Via di Capaccio (Loggia del Porcellino)

Traces of Florence's history can be found in its streets and its language. Giuseppe Lacheri made his mark on both. Not far from the Loggia del Porcellino in Piazza del Mercato Nuovo a plaque commemorates this character who was for long a lively presence in one of the most typical street markets of nineteenth-century Florence.

Lacheri may not have been a man of wealth or great learning, but his reputation was such that it is still common to hear Florentines use the expression *Egli ha ragione, i'Lachera* (He's right, Il Lachera) to put an end to a dispute – in particular, to reject the unconvincing arguments of an adversary.

Lacheri was a simple market trader in San Lorenzo, and he acquired his reputation thanks to the no-nonsense readiness with which he replied to customers and fellow traders alike. Such frankness reflects a popular culture that is still very much part of Florence, a city that prizes itself on not "mincing its words".

The text on the plaque is significant: "It was in this old square that Giuseppe Lacheri (1811–1864), known as Il Lachera, became popular. A droll market trader, he was famous for the sort of authentic Florentine wit commemorated by Collodi."

Carlo Lorenzini – *alias* Collodi, creator of *Pinocchio* – wrote this brief yet affectionate portrait of the trader: "Lachera was the very embodiment of sarcastic and wry wit, under the guise of a seller of baked pears or grape tarts, depending on the season."

Just like Collodi, the Florentines retain a fond memory of this popular market trader, of whom unfortunately no portrait survives. This plaque, raised in 2005, is a sign that within Florence – and the Loggia del Porcellino might be described as the very *heart* of Florence – popular wit survives to this day, making its mark both on the walls among which people live and on the language they use.

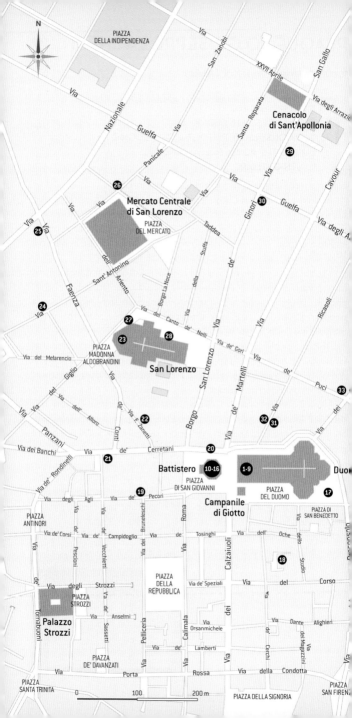

Duomo / San Lorenzo

OBSERVING THE SUN WITHIN THE CATHEDRAL

An exceptional astronomical phenomenon

Cathedral Santa Maria del Fiore
Piazza del Duomo
Hours : Monday - Wednesday from 10am to 5pm, Thursday from 10am to
3.30pm, Saturday from 10am to 4.45pm, Sunday and holidays from 1.30pm to
4. 45pm
Admission free
Solar observations with public commentary by an astronomer in June; for exact
dates visit: www.operaduomo.firenze.it
Entrance by the Porta dei Canonici (southern side of the cathedral);
tell the custodians you want to see "la meridiana"

The astronomical activity of the cathedral of Florence cannot usually be witnessed: the Capella della Croce is normally reserved for Mass and the zodiacal inscriptions on the floor are covered.

But, around four times a year, near the summer solstice (June 21), the cathedral provides an extraordinary spectacle that science buffs won't want to miss: you can observe the passage of the sun within the building itself. This feature was restored to full "working order" in 1996 and now the ecclesiastical authorities, working in conjunction with a committee dedicated to promoting public interest in astronomy, allow groups to observe the phenomenon; in theory, these groups should be limited to 150 people, but there were 250 on the day we visited. What you see is the sudden apparition of a circle of light which then can be observed moving across the floor to come to rest exactly over a circle of marble whose position was calculated in 1475 by Paolo dal Pozzo Toscanelli (1397–1482).

Apart from these special days, there is little visible trace of the astronomical activity associated with the church. During the Renaissance, astronomers were allowed to take advantage of the internal layout of the cathedral and the exceptional height of its cupola to carry out measurements that previously had been impossible. Toscanelli had assisted Brunelleschi in his calculations for the cathedral dome, and in 1475 he was allowed to install a bronze plaque (la bronzina) with an opening measuring about 5 centimetres across.

The light that passed through this opening fell to the floor of the building in the Cappella della Croce; the exact spot where it strikes at the time of the summer solstice is marked by a marble disk still visible today. In 1510, a wider circle whose diameter better corresponds to that of the ray of light was added (the original was kept out of respect for Toscanelli's work). This feature of the building was used in various types of astronomical work, including the reformation of the calendar. It has also served to study sun spots, the progression of eclipses, and the transit of Venus in front of the sun.

For more information on how such meridians work, see pag. 75.

XIMENES SUNDIAL

The highest sundial in the world

Santa Maria del Fiore cathedral
Piazza del Duomo

Sundial meridians were often located in cathedrals, whose massive size increased the distance between the point of entry of the light and the

point at which it struck the ground: the greater that distance, the more accurately scientists could calculate the angle of incidence. Another reason for the frequency of such scientific instruments within cathedrals was that the Church itself had an interest in them: they made it possible to calculate the exact date of Easter.

So, in 1754, almost 300 years after Toscanelli (see preceding double page), the Italian mathematician, engineer, astronomer and geographer Leonardo Ximenes (1716–1786) used such an opening to calculate the variations in the angle of inclination of the Earth's axis with respect to the plane of its elliptical orbit. His proposal to use the specific characteristics of the building (the height of the cupola made for unusually precise measurements) aroused the immediate interest of both civil and religious authorities.

In 1755 he obtained permission to have a marble meridian line inlaid on the floor of the Capella della Croce (this ran through the two previously installed marble disks). The angle of the solar image could be read directly from the calibrations on this line, with Ximenes' calculations finally concluding that the inclination of the Earth's axis changed by just over 30' (about one-fiftieth of a degree) per century. Modern-day astronomers put the figure at around 47'.

For Ximenes, it was essential that the observational readings be "absolute", so that they could be "transferable". This meant that he had to be able to give the precise size of all the instruments he used – for example, the height of the gnomonic opening above the floor of the cathedral. In fact, near the high altar (but not open to visitors) there is an elliptical paving stone that indicates the point that forms an exact perpendicular with the central axis of the opening. Within the stone are engraved standard measures of a *braccio fiorentino* (58.36 centimetres) and a *pied parisien* (32.48 centimetres). Ximenes had to overcome considerable difficulties in order to obtain the required precision in his measurements of the opening's height. For example, to measure the vertical distance from the opening to the floor (just under 90 metres) he used a copper chain. When this was suspended down to the floor, however, the links stretched. And even that stretching varied according to the weight the individual link was actually supporting (i.e. its position in the chain). This meant that when the chain was returned to the horizontal, it was no longer the same length. Ximenes therefore decided to measure it when suspended, using the standard measurement he chose for the purpose: the *toise parisienne* (1.95 metres). Another problem was the expansion of this metal standard due to increases in temperature. If this was not to invalidate his observations, he had to carry out all the different measurements on the same day and at the same time, allowing for the fact that the temperature within the cathedral varies depending on proximity to the lantern. The error in his final measurements was no more than 2 in 100,000 – a remarkable degree of precision for that period.

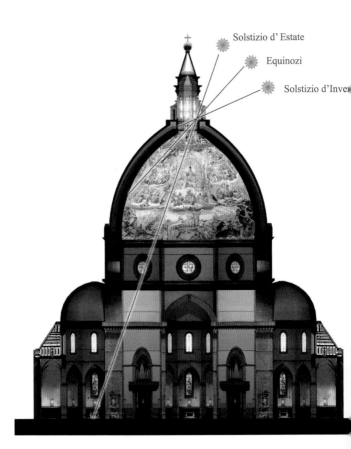

Solstizio d' Estate

Equinozi

Solstizio d'Inver

How does a meridian work?

Instead of the shadow of a gnomon, meridians use a small hole placed at a certain height, through which the Sun's light falls onto a meridian line (i.e. one aligned exactly north-south). The fact that the Sun's rays perform the function of the shadow in a traditional sundial means that the opening is sometimes referred to as a "gnomonic opening". The higher the opening, the more efficient the meridian, hence the interest in using cathedrals (see pag.77); the circumference of the hole had to be no more than one thousandth of the height above the ground. Obviously, the opening had to be installed on the south side of the building in order to let in the rays of the Sun, which lies to the south in the northern hemisphere.

The meridian line should run from the point which stands perpendicularly below the axis of the opening, not always easy to determine using the instruments available to scientists in the past (see preceding double page). The length of the line depends on the height of the opening; in some cases, where the building was not long enough to trace the entire meridian line across the floor (as was the case at Saint-Sulpice in Paris), an obelisk was added at its end, so that the movement of the Sun's rays could then be measured up the vertical. In summer, when the Sun is highest in the sky, the rays fall onto the meridian line closer to the south wall (where that line begins) they do in winter, when the Sun is lower over the horizon and the rays tend to strike towards the far end of the meridian line.

The main principle behind the working of the meridian is that at noon, solar time, the Sun is at its apex and, by definition, its rays fall straight along a line running exactly north-south. So, the exact moment when those rays strike the meridian line, which does run north-south, indicates solar noon. Furthermore, the exact place on the meridian line where that ray falls makes it possible to determine the day of the year: the point right at the beginning of the line is reached solely on the day of the summer solstice, whilst the exact end of the line is reached on the day of the winter solstice. Experience and observation meant that the meridian line could be calibrated to identify different days of the year.

Once this was done, the line could be used to establish the date of various movable feasts, such as Easter – one of the great scientific and religious uses of meridians. Similarly, could be established the different periods corresponding with the signs of the Zodiac, which explains why such signs indicated along the length of a number of meridian lines.

Why was october 4 followed immediately by october 15 in the year 1582?

The measurement of time and the origin of the meridians

The entire problem of the measurement of time and the establishment of calendars arises from the fact that the Earth does not take an exact number of days to orbit the Sun: one orbit in fact takes neither 365 nor 366 days but rather 365 days, 5 hours, 48 minutes and 45 seconds. At the time of Julius Caesar, Sosigenes of Alexandria calculated this orbit as 365 days and 6 hours. In order to make up for this difference of an extra 6 hours, he came up with the idea of an extra day every four years: thus the Julian calendar – and the leap year – came into being.

In AD 325, the Council of Nicaea established the temporal power of the Church (it had been called by Constantine, the first Roman emperor to embrace Christianity). The Church's liturgical year contained fixed feasts such as Christmas, but also movable feasts such as Easter. The latter was of essential importance as it commemorated the death and resurrection of Christ, and so the Church decided that it should fall on the first Sunday following the full moon after the spring equinox. That year, the equinox fell on March 21, which was thus established as its permanent date. However, over the years, observation of the heavens showed that the equinox (which corresponds with a certain known position of the stars) no longer fell on March 21. The 11 minutes and 15 seconds difference between the real and assumed time of the Earth's orbit around the Sun was resulting in an increasing gap between the actual equinox and March 21. By the sixteenth century, that gap had increased to ten full days and so Pope Gregory XIII decided to intervene. Quite simply, ten days would be removed from the calendar in 1582, and it would pass directly from October 4 to October 15. It was also decided, on the basis of complex calculations (carried out most notably by the Calabrian astronomer Luigi Giglio), that the first year of each century (ending in 00) would not actually be a leap year, even though divisible by four. The exceptions would fall every 400 years, which would mean that in 400 years there would be a total of just 97 (rather than 100) leap years. This came closest to making up the shortfall resulting from the difference between the real and assumed time of orbit. Thus 1700, 1800 and 1900 would not be leap years, but 2000 would...

In order to establish the full credibility of this new calendar – and convince the various Protestant nations that continued to use the Julian calendar – Rome initiated the installation of large meridians within its churches. A wonderful scientific epic had begun.

The meridian of Santa Maria del Fiore: the highest in the world

From the fifteenth to the eighteenth century almost seventy meridians were installed in churches in France and Italy. Only ten, however, have a gnomonic opening that is more than 10 metres above floor level – that height being crucial to the accuracy of the instrument:

S. S. Maria del Fiore (Florence)	90.11 m
S. Petronio (Bologna)	27.07 m
St-Sulpice (Paris)	26.00 m
Monastery of San Nicolo l'Arena (Catania, Sicily)	23.92 m
Cathedral (Milan)	23.82 m
S. Maria degli Angeli (Rome)	20.34 m
Collège de l'Oratoire (Marseille)	17.00 m
S. Giorgio (Modica, Sicily)	14.18 m
Museo Nazionale (Naples)	14.00 m
Cathedral (Palermo)	11.78 m

Why were meridians installed in cathedrals?

To make their measurements more precise, astronomers required enclosed spaces where the point admitting light was as high as possible from the ground: the longer the beam of light, the more accurately they could establish that it was meeting the floor along an exactly perpendicular plane. Cathedrals were soon recognised as the ideal location for such scientific instruments as meridians. Furthermore, the Church had a vested interest, because meridians could be used to establish the exact date of Easter.

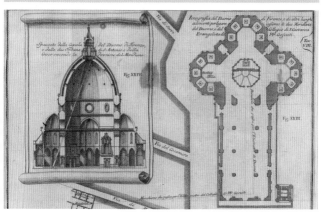

PAOLO UCCELLO'S CLOCK

Artist employed in the measurement of time

Santa Maria del Fiore cathedral
Piazza del Duomo
Monday–Wednesday from 10am to 5pm; Thursday 10am to 3.30pm; Saturday
10am to 4.45pm; Sundays and public holidays 1.30pm to 4.45pm
Admission free

Even if their name is not immediately associated with the history of clockmaking, certain great Florentine artists did play an important role in the history of time measurement. After all, they lived in a city which was the birthplace of various master clockmakers, who would make Florence one of the centres of this nascent industry for centuries. For example, the architect Filippo Brunelleschi also invented timepieces; his clock in Palazzo dei Vicari at Scarperia can still be seen today. Leonardo da Vinci may not have made clocks, but he did meticulously study their mechanisms. And it was Galileo himself who proved the isochronism of small oscillations. As for Paolo Uccello, his name is linked with the large clock that can be seen inside the cathedral over the main doorway. The original mechanism, subsequently modified a number of times over the centuries (the present one dates from 1761), was designed in 1443 by Angelo Niccolai degli Orologi, grandson of the Niccolò di Berardo who had built the clock at Palazzo Vecchio (since destroyed). Angelo's workshop was in a street that was subsequently renamed Via dell'Oriuolo (*oriuolo* being an old form of the word *orologio* – "clock"). Within the cathedral it was Paolo Uccello who painted the large circle with the 24 hours laid out in the sequence that was typical of the time – that is, what we would consider "anticlockwise" and starting from the bottom rather than the top. The first hour of the day was immediately after sunset, while the 24th corresponded to the hour of the evening Ave Maria. Thus, by beginning from the bottom, the hour at which the Sun was at its zenith corresponded to the hour at the very summit of the clock face. The Duomo clock measured out the rhythm of civic and religious life in Florence, although there were no chimes to strike individual hours. The face itself has only one clock hand – again the work of Paolo Uccello – even if the star-form design is so elaborate that you might be forgiven for thinking that there are actually three clock hands. In 1750 the clock face was adapted to what was becoming the dominant 12-hour system, later imposed as the norm under Napoleonic rule. This new system had the great advantage of cutting the maximum number of chimes from 24 to 12 (thus reducing the possibility of error for those counting each chime to tell the time). In 1968 the clock underwent painstaking restoration of the original 24-hour format. The frescoes of the evangelists to the four sides of the clock face are also by Paolo Uccello.

OLD CONSTRUCTION HOIST AT THE DUOMO

Traces of building work on the cathedral

Santa Maria del Fiore cathedral
Piazza del Duomo
Monday–Wednesday from 10am to 5pm; Thursday 10am to 3.30pm; Saturday 10am to 4.45pm; Sundays and other public holidays 1.30pm to 4.45pm
Admission free
Entrance to the cupola: Monday–Friday from 8.30am to 7pm; Saturday 8.30am to 5.40pm; first Saturday of the month 8.30am to 4pm; closed Sundays and public holidays • Admission: €6; last tickets sold 40 minutes before closing time
Warning: there are 463 steps to climb!

The construction of a cathedral is a project that involves the whole city; acting as a catalyst on the life of the community, it can generate great tensions but also curious episodes of greater or lesser historical significance. And this is particularly true if – as was the case with Santa Maria del Fiore – building work continues over centuries. This explains why the very fabric of the cathedral and the surrounding area are rich in echoes of events that helped to establish the identity of Florence.

The cupola over the choir of the cathedral was designed and built by Filippo Brunelleschi in the years 1420–1436. Given the huge dimensions of the project, a range of innovative techniques had to be used, both in the structural design of the cupola and in the handling of the thousands of tons of materials required to build it. For Brunelleschi, these technical problems offered another chance to demonstrate his genius, with the architect himself inventing lifting equipment whose power of leverage was greatly increased by carefully designed gear systems. He even invented a system for installing tables high up on the structure, thus saving time by removing the need for the workmen to come down to ground level at mealtimes.

Brunelleschi's knowledge of machine design came from clockmaking, whose secrets he had learned while serving his apprenticeship with a clockmaker. And ten years after the construction of the cupola, his gear systems would again prove useful when they served to hoist into place the sphere atop the lantern – an operation in which the young Leonardo da Vinci was involved (see the collapse of the lantern in 1600).

The finished cupola rises 35.5 metres above the drum beneath – that is, 90 metres above ground level (107 metres including the lantern). It is estimated to weigh around 37,000 tons.

There is little surviving evidence of the building work itself. Most notable are two modest hoists fitted into wooden brackets under the central vaults of two of the so-called *tribune morte* (blank tribunes). These small structures around the outside of the drum beneath the oculi served to counteract the horizontal thrust exerted by the cupola.

Outside the cathedral – at the base of the drum, facing the premises of La Misericordia (that is, at the Via de' Calzaiuoli entrance to the building) – you can see the traces of another hoist in a niche.

BULL AT THE PORTA DELLA MANDORLA

"Cuckold" door

Santa Maria del Fiore cathedral
Piazza del Duomo

I t is the Porta della Mandorla which leads to the summit of Brunelleschi's gigantic cupola, reached after 463 steep and sometimes narrow steps. Among the sculptural decoration of this doorway note the fine set of horns on the head of a bull which seems to be looking towards the house opposite him and to the left. It's said that this was the work of a waggish master mason, who placed the grim-looking bull there in order to mock a man whom all the world knew to be jealous of his young and beautiful wife.

LION NIGHTMARE ⑥

Il leone mortale

Santa Maria del Fiore cathedral
Piazza del Duomo

Another side doorway – this time on the left of the cathedral – is framed by two columns supported by a lion and lioness respectively. This is the Porta de Balla, or dei Cornacchini, and owes its name to a tragic episode.

In the fifteenth century Angelo, a neighbour of the Cornacchini family, had a terrible nightmare: he was being devoured by a lion identical to that supporting one of these two columns. The following day, to exorcise the fear caused by the nightmare, he came and put his hand within the large open mouth of the lion. Unfortunately, a large scorpion was nesting there and poor Anselmo died that very day from the sting he received on his thumb.

BLASPHEMOUS ANGEL
OF THE DUOMO

Greeting from the Angel of the Sodomites

Santa Maria del Fiore cathedral
Piazza del Duomo
First angel to the right of the doorway on the far right

Look carefully at the first angel to the right of the doorway on the far right of the Duomo's façade. All the doorways conceal a message, as was required of all entrances to a cathedral. In the arches over the openings are small sculptural groups that depict recognisable figures and recount a narrative. So far, so good. Nothing out of the ordinary; indeed, there is the usual multitude of angels and figures of greater or lesser significance.

In all Gothic cathedrals, what is striking are the masses of imaginary animals that crowd walls and roofs. However, among the angels of the Florence Duomo there is one whose gesture is, at the very least, disconcerting: there he is, clearly giving us the finger. Some – for example, David Leavitt – see this as a coded, but very clear message. This, they claim, is the Angel of the Sodomites. The records of sodomy in Florence include, for example, Dante's depiction of his own teacher, Brunetto Latini, among the circle of sodomites in hell. And other literary sources provide extensive evidence that sodomy was widespread on the banks of the Arno. However, here it is architecture itself that refers even more blatantly to the practice, with an angel directing an insult at us by mimicking an erection from the very doorway of the Duomo. The gesture may pass unobserved amidst the numerous images that crowd the doorway, but it is a blasphemy of rare impertinence.

Baccio d'Agnolo's abandoned project

"It looks like a cage for crickets," commented Michelangelo when looking up at the raised walkway that runs along only one of the eight sides of the cupola. And Baccio d'Agnolo, architect of the said walkway, was so discouraged that he did not complete the project. Unless the truth is that he himself had doubts about this "enclosure", which was intended to run as a sort of ring around the base of the cupola. The walkway would have been a spectacular construction, but it risked stunting the upward thrust of the cupola as a whole. And then there was the fact that Brunelleschi's calculations hadn't taken such an aerial construction into account, so the walkway might have compromised the statics of the whole structure. Whatever the reason, this complex project, on which work had begun ten years earlier, was abandoned in 1516, to the great satisfaction of Michelangelo and no real regrets from the city as a whole. The surviving stretch of Baccio d'Agnolo's walkway now stands as a solitary extravagance in mid-air. An odd sight, it is a reminder that the cathedral was for centuries the site of ongoing construction work, with this symbol of Florence being the object of discussions, proposals and debate.

CONCEALED SELF-PORTRAIT OF GIUSEPPE CASSIOLI

Strangled by a serpent for delivering work late

Right doorway to the Duomo
Santa Maria del Fiore cathedral
Piazza del Duomo

Not all the anecdotes associated with the cathedral refer to the Renaissance. As was to be expected of such a major church, building work on Santa Maria del Fiore would, with dozens of interruptions, continue for a long time. Perhaps rather less expected is that it was not completed until the end of the nineteenth century: the façade was only officially inaugurated on May 12 1887, that is six centuries after the laying of the first stone. And even then the doors were missing.

It was another decade before the doors for the left doorway, by Augusto Passaglia, were complete, and a further two years (1899) before the brothers Amos and Giuseppe Cassioli finished work on the right doorway.

Having been severely criticised for this delay, Giuseppe Cassioli, with a certain irony, included a self-portrait in the bronze bas-reliefs decorating his door, showing himself being strangled by a snake. It is at about eye level on the right-hand side. But even then work was unfinished.

Not until 1903 were the central doors – again the work of Augusto Passaglia – inaugurated in a ceremony attended by King Victor Emmanuel III. Then – finally! – work on the façade came to an end.

⑨

NEARBY
The Bischeri inscription

On the south side of the cathedral, near the bell tower, is an inscription just above eye level to the right of the visitors' doorway. Carved into marble, this announces the birth of a member of the Bischeri family. Due to the history of the Bischeri, the word has in Tuscan dialect become a synonym for "idiot".

When planning to build the cathedral, the authorities of the Republic of Florence had to expropriate the homes of those who lived on the selected site. Each householder was offered a reasonable price; however, the Bischeri family refused point blank and would not budge. It is said that a mysterious fire then destroyed the houses that they owned, and thus they received only a derisory sum in compensation for their now-vacant plot.

Another version has it that the Florentine authorities lost patience with them and exiled the entire family without compensation. Hence the use of their name to indicate someone who is stupid and pigheaded. Hence also the fact that the family preferred to change their name to Guadagni [Earnings]. Where Via dell'Oriulo runs into Piazza del Duomo there is a plaque with the inscription *Canto dei Bischeri*; it indicates where the family used to live.

MARBLE SOLSTITIAL MARKER

Traces of the meridian in the Baptistery

Baptistery
Piazza San Giovanni
Open from 12.15pm to 7pm; Sundays and public holidays 8.30am to 2pm;
closed January 1, Easter Sunday, September 8 and Christmas Day
Admission: €3

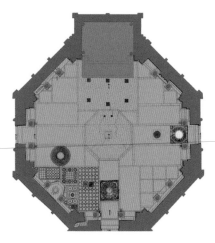

Of all the various astronomical instruments installed within Florence's ancient buildings and monuments, the oldest is actually the least well known. It is to be found within the Baptistery and comprises a large circular floor plaque of marble between the north and east doorways. The plaque bears the twelve signs of the zodiac with a Sun engraved at the centre enclosed with the Latin palindrome (a phrase that reads the same forwards and backwards): *EN GIRO TORTE SOL CICLOS ET ROTOR IGNE* ("I am the Sun. I am that wheel turned by fire whose turning turns the spheres").

This is the last trace of the solar clock which was installed in the Baptistery some time before the year 1000. The building, dating from the fourth to fifth centuries, was a Christian place of worship in the seventh century, serving as a cathedral until, in 1128, it officially became the Baptistery. Mentioned in the *Chronicles* of Flipppo Villani (1325–1407) as being on the lower edge of the lantern, a hole within a bronze plaque (no longer there) in the cupola allowed a ray of light to fall upon the signs of the zodiac that were laid out around the marble plaque.

In the thirteenth century, the marble floor was replaced by one identical to the original, but without care being taken to place the plaque in its original position; hence, as Villani explains, the solar clock no longer worked. However, the real reason for its demise was that the meridian had become obsolete due to the precession of the equinoxes*. So the hole was covered over and the solar clock was left to serve a merely decorative purpose. However, the large marble solstitial plaque is no simple "defunct machine"; it is the oldest surviving trace of Florence's centuries-old interest in the stars. Furthermore, the elegance of design and form makes it a magnificent example of the arts applied to science.

* *The precession of the equinoxes is due to the slow change in the inclination of the Earth's axis of rotation. This shift means that the axis of rotation itself actually defines a cone, completed about every 25,800 years.*

The Cabbala and the Baptistery

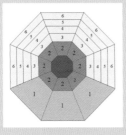

The Baptistery of San Giovanni Battista inherited the traditional forms of sacred geometry which had been used by the ancient Roman architects and were the precursors of what can be seen in Romanesque and Gothic architecture. Its floor-plan is an octagon measuring 25.6 metres in diameter, a form that is also often found in medieval baptismal fonts, which frequently stood upon an octagonal base or rested upon a "rotonda" of eight columns. St Ambrose had argued that the octagon was a symbol of the Resurrection, thus here it symbolised the eternal life which the neophyte gained when baptised. In effect, the rite of Christian baptism comprised two highly symbolic phases: immersion in and emergence from water. The immersion, now reduced to sprinkling with water, corresponds to the disappearance of a sin-laden being within the waters of death, to purification and a return to the origins of life. The emergence from water symbolises the emergence of a purified being in a state of grace, reconciled with the divine source of a new life. The Baptistery's medieval baptismal fonts stood at its centre and were decorated with geometrical motifs and the signs of the zodiac; it is said that their design had been inspired by Dante's Divine Comedy. Those fonts were then transformed in 1576 by the craftsman Bernardo Buontaleni, working at the behest of Francesco I de' Medici, and have survived to this day. The Baptistery's shape is intended to represent the eighth day (*octava dies*), that of Christ's Ascension. This is reinforced by an octagonal lamp, added in 1150. The entire spiritual universe is the subject of the mosaics in the cupola, which were added from 1270 onwards. With gold backgrounds, they comprise eight sections (one for each side of the octagon) that were in turn divided into six parts, creating 48 compartments – a distribution that reflects the numerical logic of the Kabbalah. Raban Maur (780/784? - 856), abbot of Fulda in Germany, identifies this number of 48 (6x8) as the total of the biblical prophets who were admitted to divine ministry and received direct spiritual revelations. At the top of this decorative schema is a depiction of the hierarchy of angels surmounted by a *Last Judgement*, which itself is dominated by the large figure of Christ, at whose feet are the resurrection of the dead: to the right are the Just, received into heaven by the biblical patriarchs, to the left are the damned in a demon-filled hell. A further symbolic reference to access to divine salvation is to be found in the three doors; the South Door, completed in 1336, was the work of Andrea Pisano, while the North and East Doors were the work of Lorenzo Ghiberti (the former completed in 1422, the latter begun in 1425). The number of these doors reflects the number of the Trinity, whilst their decoration is inspired by the Old and New Testaments, between whose ancient patriarchs and new apostles St John the Baptist stood as a sort of link. The decoration of each door again was conceived on the basis of a numerical logic inspired by the Kabbalah. For example, the South Door has 28 rectangular panels depicting the acts and virtues of John the Baptist. They are laid out in seven vertical columns of four compartments each in horizontal alignment and enclosed within lozenges (of a lobate form known as *compasso gotico*). The first twenty panels depict episodes from the *Life of the Baptist*, beginning on the left (1-10) and continuing on the right (11-20). Then come the personifications of the Three Theological Virtues of *Faith, Hope and Charity* (21-23), to which are added *Humility* (24), and finally the four Cardinal Virtues of *Fortitude, Temperance, Justice* and *Prudence* (25-28). On the North Door, there are again twenty-eight panels, this time depicting scenes from the New Testament, with the last two rows depicting eight saints: John, Matthew, Luke and Mark (the four Evangelists) and Ambrose, Jerome, Gregory and Augustine (the Doctors of the Church). Antonio Paolucci described this door as "the most important event in the history of Florentine art in the first quarter of the fifteenth century." The number 28 symbolises reflection within the Kabbalah: just as the moon in its cycle of 28 days reflects the light of the Sun, so it is the faithful who are to contemplate and reflect upon the images within these doors, absorbing their full meaning and thus gaining awareness of the virtues depicted therein – virtues that will lead them on the path towards the perfection of Heaven. The East Door comprises ten panels depicting scenes from the Old Testament, here rendered in perspective depth; the technique of perspective was unknown before this period. Michelangelo called this door la *Porta del Paradiso*, the name by which it is still known. The significance of the number 10 in the Kabbalah arises from the Hebrew writings that claim God created the world by means of ten creative powers (Sephiroths). Ten was also associated with the realm that he first established, Paradise, where he set the first human couple. When Man fell into original sin (the sin of sexual corruption), God gave him the Ten Commandments, so that by following them through the course of his life he might regain the Eden of the original Paradise. Ten is the number of the whole; it summarises God's creation.

TOMB OF THE ANTIPOPE JOHN XXIII

Pope or antipope?

Battistero di Firenze
Piazza San Giovanni
www.operaduomo.firenze.it
Open: 12.15pm -7pm, sunday and the first saturday of the month 8.30am-2pm
Easter Monday, aprile 25, maggio 1, Thursday, Friday and holy Saturday
8.30am-7pm
Closing: January 1, Easter, September 8, Christmas
Entrance: 4 €

Baldassare Cossa was elected Pope John XXIII by the Council of Pisa in 1410 – a council he had helped to organise and, above all, finance. He died in 1419 at Florence, a city which had been his ally.

He was however an "antipope" only until 1415, the year in which he was deposed and recognised as Pope Martin V in Rome. Having maintained his rank as bishop, he would be buried in the Florence Bap-

tistery – certainly not a place for the tomb of a heretic. Indeed, he was long considered as one of the legitimate leaders of the Church – as can be seen from the papal *Annuaries* published up to 1947 and from the mosaics in the Papal Basilica of St Paul in Rome, which include his portrait as pontiff.

However, Pope Angelo Roncalli was not of this opinion, deciding to disavow the apostolic succession of Baldassare Cossa by himself taking the name of John XXIII (a decision that raised doubts among historians). Curiously enough, Cossa's predecessor – another "antipope", Alexander V – was to see the legitimacy of his apostolic succession recognised, with the next pope to take the name Alexander being known as Alexander VI. The antipope John XXIII did not enjoy the same fate. Still, his imposing tomb remains in the Baptistery as some sort of compensation.

Antipopes: a question of legitimacy

The election of antipopes was one of the most striking symptoms of the deep conflicts within the Church; it also demonstrates the role that politics played in the choice of a pontiff. The antipopes were elected by "dissident" conclaves and were not recognised by the guardians of Roman Catholic orthodoxy, even if their situation was not always clear-cut: for example, the antipope John XXIII was buried with the full honours of his rank in one of the most prestigious places of Catholic worship – which would not have happened if he had been a heretic. The first antipope, Hippolytus, reigned from 217 to 235, in opposition to Pope Pontian, with whom he would later be reconciled. He subsequently died a martyr of the Church. Numerous antipopes reigned for only a short time, elected as the result of temporary disagreements. However, from 1378 onwards, the antipopes of Avignon formed a consolidated system of alternatives to the head of the Church in Rome. Indeed, in 1437, the antipope Benedict XIV would, according to a suggestion repeated in two historical novels (Jean Raspail's *L'Anneau du pêcheur* and Gérard Bavoux's *Le Porteur de lumière*), appoint various cardinals to secretly nominate other antipopes in order to prolong the "Avignon line". This "line" ended with Benedict XVI (1470 - 1499), but in the meantime yet another claimant to the throne of St Peter had been elected: Felix V (1439 - 1449). So, at one time, there were three putative popes. The election of antipopes came to an end after 1499, but the practice probably contributed to the calls for ecclesiastical renewal that inspired the Protestant Reformation.

GHIBERTI'S CONCEALED SELF-PORTRAIT

Signature of the creator of the Porta del Paradiso

Porta del Paradiso
Baptistery

There are various portrait busts concealed within the doors of the Baptistery, whose very weight has become legendary: Galileo himself commented that even if they were pushed shut very gently, the whole building would tremble the moment they struck the threshold. This masterpiece by Lorenzo Ghiberti, which Michelangelo dubbed the *Porta del Paradiso* (Gate of Paradise), contains a self-portrait of the artist himself. Bald and with a wry expression, he is to be seen in the frame of the left-hand door at the fifth level (the levels are read left to right and from the bottom upwards). At the same level, on the right-hand door, is a portrait of Bartoluccio Ghiberti, his presence here a tribute from his adoptive son and pupil Lorenzo.

Recycled stones

Just like other cathedrals – for example, that in Pisa – the Florence Baptistery (originally a cathedral) was built using masonry, sometimes dressed stones, taken from elsewhere. This would explain the incongruous presence – near ground level, to the left of the north doors – of a sculptured frieze decorated with a naval scene and some figures. It probably came from a Roman sarcophagus.

Another recycled stone is to be seen to the upper right of the east doors, facing the Duomo. Here, a curious inscription that has nothing to do with the cathedral is set into the wall.

TRACES OF THE COLUMNS ⑬
OF SANTA REPARATA CATHEDRAL

Vestiges of old Florence

On the pavement between the Baptistery and the Duomo, five sets of stone slabs stand out from the others because of their different colour and pattern. These indicate where the columns of an earlier cathedral dedicated to St Reparata used to stand. Construction of Santa Maria del Fiore (the Duomo) began in 1296 on the same site. Traces of the ancient structure can be seen in the crypt.

THE ELM TREE
AND THE SAN ZENOBIO COLUMN

Commemorating the passage of a miracle-working corpse

Piazza Duomo, opposite the left doorway of Santa Maria del Fiore cathedral

It is to be hoped that now Piazza del Duomo is rid of the traffic that was choking it, San Zenobio's column will be restored to its rightful place within the city centre. To date, this granite monument surmounted by an iron cross has made no more impression than a street lamp – particularly as there is nothing particularly ostentatious about it. However, the height of the column and its position – between the Baptistery and the Duomo – are clear indications that it once had very precise meaning and importance. St Zenobio (337– 417) was Florence's first bishop. He was credited with a wide range of miracles, including the resurrection of the son of a French pilgrim (a miracle that is commemorated by a plaque on the façade of Palazzo Valori e Altoviti). Some years after his death, when his body was being transferred from San Lorenzo to Santa Reparata (which stood on the site of the present cathedral), the bier happened to brush against a dead elm tree whose branches suddenly began to put forth shoots. Immediately this was claimed as a posthumous miracle. Tradition has it that all this occurred on January 26 429, although we have no date for the raising of the column to commemorate the miracle. Still, we do know that the original column was swept away by the floods of 1333 and then rebuilt soon afterwards. Though there is an inscription on the column – plus a carving of an elm tree – the name of Zenobio means nothing to modern-day Florentines, and even less to tourists. They all pass by this simple yet fairly obvious monument without realising that it bears witness to a story that is an integral part of the very identity of Florence.

What became of the wood of the miraculously revived elm?

The wood itself became a precious relic, used to make the crucifix in the church of San Giovannino e dei Cavalieri (in Via San Gallo) and to provide the panel for a painting of the Miracle of San Zenobio by an artist known as Il Maestro del Bigallo. Zenobio was so popular that, together with St Antonino Pierozzi, he became the patron saint of the diocese of Florence.

TRACES OF ANCIENT UNITS OF MEASUREMENT IN THE BAPTISTERY

It's a foot!

Piazza del Duomo

Before the advent of the metre, the arms and feet of sovereigns were often the bases for standard units of measurement. To make these units known to merchants and citizens, these lengths were reproduced on stone slabs and plaques that were then placed on public display. Some of these can still be seen: curious rectangles engraved in stone on the two columns that flank the south doors of the Baptistery.

The column on the left has two rectangles, one within the other, whose function is yet to be explained. However, on the column on the right, the simple, larger, rectangle represents a "Lombard foot". Introduced by King Liutprand (690?–744), this new unit of 38 centimetres by 51.5 centimetres was part of the arsenal of regulations intended to unify the Italian peninsula under the often resented rule of the Lombards. For example, these rulers often clashed with the papacy. Tradition has it that Liutprand himself was 1.73 metres tall – an exceptional height for the time – and that his right foot measured 25.4 centimetres and his left 26.1 centimetres; hence the measure of 51.5 centimetres, the sum of the two. However, these precise figures were disproved when Liutprand's actual remains were discovered in his tomb within San Pietro in Ciel d'Oro, a church in Pavia, his capital, and the king was shown to have been of average height. Still, a thousand years after his rule, Liutprand's foot continued to be used as a unit of measurement in some Italian cities.

What preceded the metric system?

On July 28 1861 Italy officially adopted the metric system. Before that, each province – or even city – had its own units of measurement, sometimes based upon the size of a monarch's foot or arm or hand. This confusion explains why such standards were often displayed in public places, primarily markets, where vendors and customers could consult them. Some of these old units of measurement can still be seen in Volterra and Barga. In Florence, the most commonly used units were the *braccio fiorentino* (58.4 centimetres) and the *canna agrimensoria* (2.92 metres). The Florentine foot (*piede fiorentino*) was the same length as the *pied parisien* (32.48 centimetres). The latter had become something of a standard measure throughout Europe thanks to the renown enjoyed by the architects of France's Gothic cathedrals.

BROKEN PISAN COLUMNS

A gift of Pisa

The broken porphyry columns on either side of the Baptistery doorway seem to have been left there by mistake, but they were gifts presented to Florence by the city of Pisa in gratitude for its help against Lucca in 1117. Although damaged in transit, they were nevertheless set in place to avoid wounding Pisan sensibilities, as relations between Florence and Pisa were not as cordial as they might have been.

WHERE THE CATHEDRAL LANTERN ⑰ CRASHED TO THE GROUND

La lanterna caduta dalla cattedrale

In the middle of the grey paving slabs behind the cathedral there is a round plaque in white marble. This unidentified marker in itself identifies the place where the lantern atop the cathedral crashed to the ground on February 17 1600. This was no ordinary incident of structural damage, for the lightning on this occasion had brought down two tons of building materials, with the gilded bronze ball and cross alone weighing some eighteen quintals. Fortunately nobody was injured, but the noise echoed throughout the city, with pieces of the lantern subsequently being found as far away as Via dei Servi. The lantern, the work of Andrea del Verrocchio, had been raised to the top of the cathedral in 1468, using special machinery designed for the occasion by Leonardo da Vinci. And after the collapse, Grand Duke Ferdinando I hurriedly took measures to have the damage repaired and the lantern restored. Just two years later, it – together with ball and cross – was back in place. However, the grand duke did more than just trust the skill of his engineers. In agreement with the archbishop, he sought divine protection for the restored lantern by having two small lead containers set within the arms of the cross, each containing precious holy relics and Latin inscriptions that invoked protection against lightning. To prevent any future such accidents, the lantern is nowadays protected by a lightning conductor.

TORRE DELLA PAGLIAZZA

Small private museum in a round tower

Hotel Brunelleschi
Piazza Elisabetta 3
Tel: 055 27370
Free admission on prior booking with the hotel: info@hotelbrunelleschi.it

Numerous tower residences survive within the city, most still inhabited or incorporated within other buildings; indeed, you could follow an itinerary from one tower to another that would take you across the city as across a chessboard. However, only one of these towers is round, and it stands in a small square just a short walk from the Duomo. This exceptional shape may be because the original construction was Byzantine, being built by Greek soldiers while they were defending the city against the Goths; built on the site of the *piscina* – or water basin – of Roman thermal baths, the tower was supposedly intended as an addition to the city's fortifications. However, some claim that the structure dates from a few decades later and was built by the Lombards. Whereas the puzzle of its origin may perhaps be insoluble, we do know something of the vicissitudes the tower has passed through. For a time it was used as a female prison; the *pagliazza* ("straw") refers to the material used as bedding in the cells. Then it was converted into the bell tower for the church of San Michele alle Trombe, before almost totally disappearing when it was incorporated into a building used as housing and warehouses.

More recently, the tower has been converted into a hotel. But far from involving some cheerless "updating", this superb restoration/conversion by Italo Gamberini has stripped away the building that once blocked the view of the tower and highlighted its circular form, as well as its place within the context of the piazza (itself now enjoying new life thanks to full street lighting). The restoration work revealed that the tower's foundations date back to the Romans and the end result elegantly highlights the medieval style of the structure. Inside, a remarkable little museum has been installed, which is not restricted to hotel guests and gives access to the underground area where you can admire the vaults and undressed stone walls. As well as the remnants of the Roman baths, the museum has a fine collection of pottery and fragments dating from the Roman era (first century AD), together with objects manufactured in later periods; there are even some seventeenth-century ceramics from Montelupo. All these archaeological pieces were found during the on-site excavation and restoration work. Quite apart from the artistic value of its artefacts, this unique museum is a fine example of the historic stratifications to be found within – and under – a Florentine building.

PRIVATE MUSEUM OF THE CASA DEL TESSUTO ⑲

An unknown museum

Via dei Pecori 20-24r • Tel: 055 15961

Two brothers with the delightful names of Romolo and Romano Romoli – direct descendants of the Egisto Romoli who founded the Casa del Tessuto (Home of Textiles) in 1929 – have transformed this city-centre shop into a space where there is always something going on. This is not only somewhere to find the very best textiles, but twice a week it also offers lessons for young couturiers and pupils from all over the world. There are also courses and talks on the history of the city.

The business also owns a real gem: a small museum illustrating the history of textiles. The collection includes a precious sixteenth-century weaving loom, various ancient scissors and pins, scales and numerous other instruments, plus a vast assortment of thread and bobbins. There is more than enough to offer a fascinating insight into the history of fabric-making, plus such wonderful curiosities as peacock-feather fabric.

WROUGHT-IRON ROSICRUCIAN ARMS

Secret meeting-place of the Rosicrucians

Restaurant Buca San Giovanni
Piazza San Giovanni, 8
Tel: 055 287612

This is a typical Florentine *buca* – literally meaning "hole" – the term used in the city for basement restaurants. The rooms here were once part of the sacristy of the Baptistery, which gives you some idea of their historic importance; the restaurant's premises are in fact listed. Certain furnishings date from the Middle Ages and the Renaissance – for example, the altar which has been converted into the restaurant bar, various decorations and coats of arms on the walls and a fresco (in the main room) which is attributed to the Giotto school. Rich in a sense of history, the whole underground space has a mysterious atmosphere. It is no great surprise that the followers of Rosicrucianism, in the first half of the twentieth century, should have chosen this as their secret meeting-place. The fact that the rites of this confraternity were celebrated here is confirmed by a detail which may not be apparent to the layman but is immediately clear to the initiated: a wrought-iron grille featuring the symbol of the Rosicrucians.

Rosicrucians: an Order of esoteric and mystical Christianity

The name of this esoteric Order comes from that of a German elder who lived around 1460 and was known as Christian Rosenkreutz (Christian Rose-Cross). Together with twelve disciples deeply versed in Christian mysticism, he set up an Order dedicated to the study of the religious and scientific learning of the day. Having established themselves in the south of Europe, these scholar-mystics came into contact with the spiritual and cultural learning of the Islamic world – in particular, with Sufism. These contacts remained close for a long time, thus creating a spiritual link between East and West. Tradition has it that the Rosicrucians had superhuman powers thanks to their profound knowledge of hermetism and alchemy; that they knew how to create the philosopher's stone; that they spoke directly to God, Christ, the saints and the angels; and that through these contacts they learned divine wisdom and the secrets of immortality. Their reputation for supernatural miracle-working powers continues to this day, without it being clear where reality ends and fantasy begins. The Rosicrucians very quickly faded into anonymity from the fifteenth century onwards, becoming a secret society. Indeed, no new member was accepted before the death of an existing member – thus keeping the numbers equal to 1+12, on the model of Christ and his twelve Apostles. In

1614 a work written in German (with the Latin title *Fama Fraternitatis*) was attributed to Christian Rosenkreutz, though its actual author was the theologian Johannes Valentinus Andreae (1586–1654), who was supposedly the spokesman of the Order of Rosicrucians and signed himself as its "Grand Master". He describes the origins, history and mission of the Rosicrucians, who were striving to restore primordial Christianity and rid the Church of the secular vices to which it had fallen prey. When Freemasonry evolved in the eighteenth century, it embraced Rosicrucianism, establishing in 1761 the 18th degree of *Prince of the Rose Cross* or *Knight of the Pelican* – a strictly Christian division (the bird being a Christian symbol of charity, abnegation and sacrifice).

FACE ON SANTA MARIA MAGGIORE CHURCH

21

A priest's petrified head?

Church of Santa Maria Maggiore
Via de' Cerretani

It's still there, looking out of a window that is not a window, watching who knows what from the upper side wall of Santa Maria Maggiore church in Via de' Cerretani. It isn't trying to hide, yet to see this stone head you have to look upwards. Depicting a woman, it was undoubtedly carved around 1327, the year when the astrologist Francesco Stabili – better known as Cecco D'Ascoli – was condemned to be burned at the stake. Just before the execution, a priest claimed to know the details of the pact the astrologist was said to have made with the devil. Satan, according to the cleric, had assured Francesco that he would escape all danger if he took a sip of water. "Above all, don't give him anything to drink," he urged, thus imposing a further torture on the wretched man condemned to die in the flames.

In response, Stabili is said to have told the priest: "And you… you'll never move your head from there!" Immediately the cleric's head turned to stone, becoming set within the wall where you can still see it.

Inevitably, this image of a head perched so high up on the walls of a church has over the centuries generated the most unlikely urban legends. One tells of a market gardener who brought into town a bell she could use to warn all those who didn't live within the city that the gates were about to close. Another version says that the bell was rung so that the gates could be reopened for those who were late. Whatever the truth, the Florentines are said to have commemorated this donor by having her face carved on the church wall. Another story goes that this is the head of a woman who turned to stone when cursed by the condemned man she was mocking as he was being led to his execution.

You can make up any story you wish, with this face ultimately proving only one thing: the stones of Florence are so soulful that legends are bound to arise around them.

Where Leonardo da Vinci's Mona Lisa was hidden and then recovered

It is no accident that the hotel at No. 2 Via Panzani is called "La Gioconda", because it was here – under the bed in Room 20 – that police discovered Leonardo's famous *Mona Lisa*, which had been stolen from the Louvre by an Italian nationalist who wanted the world's most famous painting to be returned to his fatherland (on payment to himself, that is). Once recovered, the painting was returned to the French State, which is undoubtedly the rightful owner of the work – not something that can necessarily be said of the pieces appropriated during the Napoleonic campaigns. The only trace of the painting in Florence is the name of this hotel, previously the Hotel Tripoli.

MUSEO DI CASA MARTELLI

22

House of marvels

Via Ferdinando Zannetti, 8
Open Thursday from 2pm to 7pm, Saturday 9am to 2pm, and the first, third
and fifth Sundays of the month 9am to 2pm
Tel: 055 216725
www.bargellomusei.beniculturali.it

What happens if a patrician mansion, concealed in a narrow street in the city centre, has no private garden? At Casa Martelli, the problem was solved by painting a salon to look like a large open-air garden. The visual effect of this multicoloured fresco, with its profusion of balustrades, fountains and panoramic views, is as exhilarating as any *trompe l'œil*. But the garden room isn't the only highlight of the museum, which holds paintings by Brueghel the Younger, Luca Giordano, Piero di Cosimo, Salvator Rosa, Beccafumi and other great masters. All the rooms have been conceived as "events" in their own right: the yellow lounge and the red lounge, the "Pucci boudoir" with its "grottoes", the bathroom with its bucolic scenes, a spectacular grand staircase, the ballroom, the chapel and the impressive picture gallery. As in the Pitti Palace's Palatine Gallery, numerous canvases are displayed in this large first-floor room: they cover the walls completely, with some unexpected juxtapositions. The current appearance of this residence dates back to the early eighteenth century, when the Martelli family commissioned architect Bernardino Ciurini, painters Vincenzo Meucci, Bernardo Minozzi and Niccolò Contestabile, and stucco artist Giovan Martino Portogalli, to create a circular itinerary to impress their guests. The uniqueness of Casa Martelli is not only due to the quality of its art collection, but the theatrical way that the works are displayed by category and dominant colour scheme. Every room has a frescoed ceiling with rigorous iconography that tells a story; complemented with period furniture and tapestries. The Martelli family was among the most important in the city, enjoying close contacts with the Medicis and the great Florentine artists. Treasures such as Donatello's *David* and the coats of arms of the House of Martelli were exhibited in their home over a long period before being transferred to the Museo Nazionale del Bargello. Other works must have been dispersed in 1986, when the last of the Martelli line, Francesca, bequeathed the palazzo to the Curia of Florence, which sold it to the Italian state in 1998.

23

HERMETISM AND THE TOMB OF LORENZO DE' MEDICI

A hidden message

Medici Chapel
Church of San Lorenzo
Tel: 055 214042 (Opera Medicea Laurenziana)
Open: weekdays 10am-5pm
Entrance: 2.50 €, free up to 6 years
Disabled access

In the Medici Chapel within the Church of San Lorenzo stands the mo- numental tomb of Lorenzo de' Medici, Duke of Urbino (1492–1519). Few of those who visit it realise that this is the burial place of the grandson of the greatest patron of occult learning in Renaissance Florence, Lorenzo il Magnifico. Nor is it widely known that there is concealed significance to the artwork of the tomb itself, designed by Michelangelo. The artist began work in 1519, dedicating himself to the task right up to his de- parture for Rome in 1534, before the completion of the initial project. During his younger years, Michelangelo is known to have studied alchemy and alchemical symbolism figures in the tombs, with the male and female statues – of *Dawn* and *Dusk* or *Day* and *Night* – embodying the begin- ning and end of the hermetist *Magnum opus*, the return to a primordial androgynous state, a perfect synthesis of man and woman. Interestingly, the three figures on the tomb – Lorenzo himself and the figure of the Man

and Woman – form a perfect triangle and thus express the perfection of the Body Present (Lorenzo), the Absent Soul (Dusk) and the Free Spirit (Dawn). One thus has the two universal periods of activity and repose which underlie all life, regulating the cycles of existence – that which the Hindus refer to as *manvantara* (action) and *pralaya* (inertia) and which are here represented by Day and Night. In the traditional symbolism of Day as derived from Jewish thought, Creation lasted six days, whilst the seventh day symbolises eternal life. In the second *Book of Esdras*, also known as the *Ascension of Isaiah*, the soul is freed from the body and undertakes a journey that corresponds to the six days of the Creation of the World and the seventh day that corresponds to God's day of rest. Thus, the soul must pass through seven heavens. Each day, it experiences the creation of Self through the different creations of God, so Day symbolises a "stage in the ascension of the spirit". Another rabbinical exegesis of *Genesis* sees the seventh day not as that of the Lord's Rest after his work of Creation – God cannot be tired – but rather as an instant when God deliberately ceased to intervene in the world, an instant when he surrendered command of and responsibility for the Universe to Man, so that humankind could make itself worthy to one day receive the Creator, who would come to live together with his Creation. Thus, the seventh day symbolises a time of action, of a Humanity left to its own devices; it is the time of responsibility and culture, seen in opposition to Nature, which was created in six days and then handed over to mankind for them to develop their own activity. It is also seen in opposition to the eighth day, which will be the day of Renovation, when Creator and Created will be reunited in a Universe of perfect harmony. The traditional symbolism of night sees it as a period of gestation, of the development of the potential which will then emerge into day as a manifestation of life. To enter night is to return to the phase of the indeterminate, the indefinite – to pre-existence. Like all symbols, there is a dual aspect to night: that of a period of shadows and darkness, within which ferments all future life, and that of the period of preparation for the day, when the light of life will break forth. In mystical theology, night also symbolises the disappearance of all distinct knowledge, of that which can be analysed and expressed; it is a time when the senses are denied access to the physical bases for knowledge. In other words, as a time of obscurity, or subjectivity, night is a time for the purification of the spirit, with its emptiness and deprivation corresponding to the purification and revitalisation of the memory. The aridness and dryness are themselves a reference to the purification of desires and affections based upon the senses – and even of the highest aspirations; sleep purifies all of these and brings with it renewed vigour. Night is the time when things cannot be seen; day is when they are made manifest. Above them, the genius of the spirit (embodied in Lorenzo de' Medici) meditates the secret thoughts of the elevated soul.

"POSTERS" AT PALAZZO VIVIANI

Baroque cartelloni in honour of Galileo

Via Sant'Antonio 11

This curiosity is ideal if you have half an hour to spare before your train leaves: just a short walk from the station of Santa Maria Novella, the narrow and bustling Via Sant'Antonio near the San Lorenzo market contains Palazzo Viviani, which is known as Palazzo dei Cartelloni because of its rather strange façade. Viviani was a famous seventeenth-century mathematician and he had the front of the building covered with three inscribed "posters" (*cartelloni*): one to either side and a smaller one in the middle. The Latin texts are by Viviani himself and describe and celebrate the astronomical discoveries and inventions of Galileo: the telescope, the "Medici planets" (actually moons of Jupiter), Sun spots, the resistance of solids, projectile trajectory, a proposed

solution to the problem of calculating longitude at sea. These are all depicted in the bas-reliefs that surmount the main doorway, together with a bust of the great astronomer by the sculptor Giovan Battista Foggini.

But Viviani did not use the *cartelloni* simply to praise Galileo's scientific achievements; he was also concerned to stress his faith and moral probity. Hence, these inscriptions have something of the air of a political manifesto. Having died while still suspected of heresy, Galileo had not even had the right to a proper funerary monument, and two centuries later he was still susceptible to contemptuous attacks by the Church.

Another curiosity is that this palazzo seems to have been built on the site of the home of the Del Giocondo family, who commissioned Leonardo da Vinci's *Mona Lisa*, also known as *La Gioconda* after the sitter's family name.

TEMPLAR CHURCH OF SAN JACOPO IN CAMPO CORBOLINI

A hidden gem

Istituto Lorenzo de' Medici campus
Via Faenza, 43
Request a visit at the university entrance

At the end of Via Faenza, almost at the junction with Via Nazionale, a treasure lies behind an ancient iron gate.

Founded in 1206 by the Knights Templar Order, the church of San Jacopo in Campo Corbolini became home to the Order Knights Templar after their its proscription and excommunication by Rome.

Although normally closed to the public, so long as you ask for permission, to enter you can visit this church on the Florentine campus of the Lorenzo de' Medici (LdM) institute.

After decades of neglect, thise church was restored has recently been restored from the ground up and has now recovered its former splendour. All the specially commissioned works of art have been replaced put back in their original locations, offering the unique experience of seeing for yourself a church furnished with its original paintings, sculptures and inscriptions.

Entering through the side door, the first thing you see is a magnificent crucifix in the style of Brunelleschi, then a massive altarpiece by Ridolfo del Ghirlandaio and a fresco by Taddeo Gaddi, as well as the frescoes of the main chapel.

Note the perfection of the garment worn by the first woman on the right in the great *Beheading of John the Baptist* by Filippo Paladini (first chapel to the left of the high altar).

The chapel's masterpiece is at the end of the nave on the right, which houses one of the most beautiful sculptures to have been preserved in Florence: on the right of the high altar, the exceptional tombstone of Luigi Tornabuoni.

The sculptor is unknown, but the artist's skill is unrivalled. Note the texture of the marble cushion on which the knight rests, so beautifully carved that it seems almost real.

SIGNS INDICATING THE NEAREST AIR-RAID SHELTERS

Capital "R" points the way

Junction of Via Panicale and Via Chiara
Entrance to arcades of Piazza del Mercato Centrale

The few apparently incomprehensible "R" signs still marking the walls of some Florentine buildings are relics of the Second World War. These signs were vital as they indicated the nearest air-raid shelters: the white capital "R" (for *rifugio* – refuge or shelter) on a black background was flanked by an arrow pointing the way. In San Lorenzo there's one between Via Panicale and Via Chiara, and another on the other side of Piazza del Mercato Centrale. There was a refuge in the nearby San Lorenzo church. These "R" signs are worth preserving before they disappear for ever.

The only plaque commemorating the bombing of Florence is in Via Mannelli, at the corner of Via Fra' Paolo Sarpi, near Campo di Marte railway station. It bears the names of victims of the September 25 1943 air raid, the most devastating of all, in which 215 people lost their lives.

MONUMENT TO ANNA DE' MEDICI ㉗

Last descendant of the Medici family

Via del Canto de' Nelli

Behind the basilica of San Lorenzo is a monument that is rather different to all the others and yet still passes almost unnoticed. The regal and confident woman seated here in an almost flirtatious pose is however commemorated every 18 February (the anniversary of her death in 1743) by a procession that ends at this monument. Thus the city pays its respects to Anna Maria Luisa de' Medici (also known as Ludovica), princess, Elector Palatine and the last descendant of the Medici family, whose death marked the end of that prestigious dynasty.

As can be seen from the letters in which Anna Maria berated her uncle Francesco Maria, cardinal and governor of Siena, for his dissolute lifestyle, this was a woman with a mind of her own, well capable of playing the role she had to adopt as the centuries-old history of the Medici came to an end. She herself had no children, left infertile by the syphilis caught from her husband, Johannes Karl Wilhelm, Elector Palatine. And she was no more successful in providing an heir for the dynasty when she arranged the marriage of her younger brother, Giovanni Gastone, the last grand duke: he quickly got rid of his wife to give free rein to his homosexuality. As there was to be no next generation of Medici, Anna Maria resigned herself to complying with the decision of the European powers of the day that her possessions should pass to the Habsburg-Lorraine family. However, in doing so she imposed a condition that revealed her foresight: known as the "Family Pact", this forbade anyone to "remove from the capital of the State collections, paintings, statues, libraries, jewelleries and other precious objects", thus guaranteeing that these treasures would continue to adorn the Grand Duchy of Tuscany to the benefit of its inhabitants and the wonder of visitors. And what an act of foresight it was! For the artistic heritage of the Grand Duchy would be the main resource of Tuscany and the city of Florence for centuries to come. Thus the honour that the city pays to Anna de' Medici each year is well deserved. What is rather less deserved is the rather casual siting of her monument.

28

CEILING OF THE OLD SACRISTY

Painted stars immortalising a specific date

Church of San Lorenzo
Piazza San Lorenzo
Tel: 055 214042 (Opera Medicea Laurenziana)
Open Monday–Friday from 10am to 5pm
Admission €2.50; free for children under 6 years
Accessible to those of restricted mobility

The star-studded fresco on the cupola of the old sacristy at San Lorenzo captures the appearance of the night sky on a specific date. Exactly the same arrangement of heavenly bodies is to be seen within the cupola of the Pazzi Chapel in Santa Croce church (see p. 196), which is all the more extraordinary as the works were commissioned for two different places by two different families (the Medici and the Pazzi respectively). The relation between these two night skies long remained a mystery, but recent restoration work and detailed study of the position of the planets and stars, of the ecliptic and its angle, have made it possible to identify the specific night depicted.

The gilding and rich turquoise colour of this fine nocturnal view celebrate July 4 1442, the day of the arrival in Florence of René of Anjou, the man who – it was hoped – would lead a new crusade against the Infidel. Among his various titles (King of Sicily, King of Hungary, Duke of Bar, King of Anjou and Lorraine, Count of Guise and so on), René – who was the son of the Queen of Spain and brother-in-law to the King of France – possessed a title that was even richer in evocative power: King of Jerusalem. Furthermore, in 1442, René was 33 years old, the same age as Christ when he died on the Cross. However, the hoped-for crusade was not all a question of religion: the Holy Land at the time attracted the interest of various great Florentine families, who were bankers to the papacy, Guelf in allegiance (like René himself) and well-versed in overseas trade.

This "fixed" night sky was not created solely with a celebratory function but was also rich in hermetic significance (see p. 196-197). In effect, it was intended to draw on the celestial energy of Jerusalem and "crystallise" it within the vault of the sacristy. The maintenance of this energy would thus support Florence's claim to the heritage of ancient Jerusalem and at the same time justify its temporal ambitions. The fresco has been attributed to Giuliano d'Arrigo – known as *Il Pesello* – who was famous for his paintings of animals. However, such a prodigious scheme also required the services of a highly skilled astronomer: Paolo dal Pozzo Toscanelli (1397–1482), who was an eminent Florentine scientist as well as being "astrologist" to Cosimo de' Medici and a friend of Filippo Brunelleschi (architect of both cupolas). These relations between scientists and artists give an insight into the fervent religious life of fifteenth-century Florence, and partly explain the interest of these two astronomical frescoes. They are not just expressions of artistic skill but an assertion of the divinatory role of astronomy: the stars indicate "the way", while the architectural form – in particular, the curved vault of a cupola – is seen as creating a chamber of meditation that can enclose the cosmic forces capable of exerting an influence on earthly events.

29

LOCOMOTIVE WITH THE FENZI COAT OF ARMS

Memories of the first Tuscan railway, linking Florence to Livorno

Palazzo Fenzi
Via San Gallo, 10

In the iconography of the coats of arms of Florentine palazzi, there are the usual fleur-de-lis, Medici spheres, weapons, animals and towers, following the traditional rules of heraldry. But Palazzo Fenzi has a unique touch: above the grand entrance to what is now Florence University's Faculty of Geography, the family symbol, carved in stone, is like a strange traveller's postcard. Two imposing statues of disturbingly sardonic satyrs hold up the balcony overhead.

Between them is the Fenzi coat of arms bordered by two other imaginary creatures (griffins) and surmounted by the Florentine fleur-de-lis. But the image in the centre of the stone deviates from the typical iconography of Tuscan palazzo façades. To the right is a meticulous depiction of Brunelleschi's dome; to the left, a lighthouse overlooking the sea, which most experts will recognize as the former tower of Livorno; and between them a locomotive on rails.

This nineteenth-century icon represents the fortune made by the engineer Emanuele Fenzi, who built the first Tuscan railway – known as the Leopolda, in honour of Grand Duke Leopold II of Tuscany – which opened in 1844 and linked Florence to the port of Livorno. Today, this railway map in stone is a flamboyant yet appropriate symbol for the entrance to the university faculty.

The façade of this beautiful palazzo is also notable for a variety of window styles – "kneeling" (because of the shape of the supports) on the ground floor, tympana on the first floor, architraves on the second – and for the magnificent bronze turtles that support the window grilles on the ground floor, rendered with so much detail that they seem real.

Fenzi was also associated with the construction of the Chianti tramway, a steam locomotive line linking Florence to the heart of the Chianti-producing areas such as San Casciano in Val di Pesa and Greve in Chianti. Brought into service stage by stage from 1890 onwards, it remained in operation for forty-five years until it was axed on July 31 1935.

CANTO ALLE *MACINE* PLAQUE

(30)

Old traces of River Mugnone in the city centre

Via Guelfa, at the corner of Via de' Ginori

The plaque here identifies this street corner as *Canto alle Macine*. In fact, an old water mill (*macine*) used to stand at the corner (*canto*) of these two roads. Nowadays there is no trace of the mill or of the water course – the Mugnone – that powered it. This tributary of the Arno used to run through the centre of the city along a course from Piazza della Libertà along Via de' Ginori to Via San Gallo. This would explain why the location of Calandrino's house in Boccaccio's *Decameron* (Day VIII, 3, 50) is given as just by the *Canto alle Macine*; it is here that this character returns from Porta San Gallo, convinced that he has found a stone that makes him invisible. But in Via San Gallo it is the Mugnone that has ended up invisible, having been rerouted each time Florence's city walls were expanded. At the time of the fourth ring of walls dating from 1078 – those which Dante describes as "the ancient ramparts" – the Mugnone flowed through Piazza San Marco then on to Via Cerretani, Via Rondinelli (its sharp angle favoured the drainage of the waters which here formed a marsh, recorded in the name of the present-day Via Panzani (*pantano* = marsh), then along the route of Via Tornabuoni into the Arno. In 1175 the water course was rerouted towards Via San Gallo – hence the *Canto alle Macine* – from where it flowed towards Via de' Fossi (the name refers to the moats – *fossi* – of the former ramparts) and entered the Arno at a spot between Ponte alla Carraia and the church of Ognissanti. The course of the river was altered again in 1283 and in 1333, to follow the route of the present-day Viale Spartaco Lavagnini and Viale Strozzi; you can still see, spanning a dry river bed, the bridge of the old Porta Faenza city gateway, which was incorporated within the Fortezza da Basso in the sixteenth century. Nowadays, the course of the Mugnone lies even further west, along the route of Viale Milton and Viale Redi, emptying into the Arno near Ponte all'Indiano.

SALETTA GONNELLI (31)

Bibliophiles' paradise

Libreria Antiquaria Gonnelli
Via Ricasoli, 6
Tel: 055 216835

First opened in 1875 and now exclusively dealing in rare books, Gonnelli's has always been more than an antique shop. Beyond the rooms of the bookshop itself – a temple to antique books – there is a real gem that is largely unknown to the non-bibliophile: the Saletta Gonnelli. Beneath elegant Renaissance vaults above simple columns, this small exhibition space is set back from the windows that give onto Via Ricasoli and is used solely for exhibitions of books, period prints and sometimes even paintings. It was thanks to this space that the bookshop, over time, became a key point of reference for the *Macchiaioli* group of Florentine and Neopolitan painters (*macchia* = patches – of colour). As well as exhibitions of work by such artists as Giovanni Fattori, Tito Conti and Giorgio de Chirico, the place also saw the launch of Futurist literary reviews and attracted such intellectuals as Benedetto Croce, Giuseppe Papini and Gabriele D'Annunzio, with publishing activities ranging over a variety of journals and scholarly works. Nowadays, the Saletta Gonnelli, within the shadow of the Duomo, remains dedicated to the enjoyment of books with its unique volumes of writing, pictorial and graphic arts. All in all, a museum for bibliophiles.

A BOMB AS A CREST

32

Symbol of the famous Accademia degli Infuocati

Teatro Niccolini
Via Ricasoli, 5 (theatre closed at present)

A short distance from Piazza del Duomo, a small grille on the right-hand side of Via Ricasoli covers a doorway surmounted by two lanterns. This is the elegant entrance to a theatre that has been closed for some years now: Teatro Niccolini, which used to be called Teatro del Cocomero after the street (itself subsequently renamed Via Ricasoli). It was this earlier name that French writer Stendhal uses when discussing the theatre in his travel book *Rome, Naples et Florence en 1817*, mentioning in passing the peculiarity of Florentine pronunciation that turns "cocomero" into "*hohomero*". At the centre of the façade, the entrance to the theatre is also marked by a decidedly unusual crest carved over the cornice. When you look closely, you see that this is not a watermelon as many Florentines claim – misled by the fact that *cocomero* in Italian means "watermelon" – but a sort of incendiary bomb, shown in the act of exploding. A rather incongruous presence in an age increasingly obsessed by the security of public places, this was the symbol of the famous Accademia degli Infuocati (Academy of the Enflamed) which was founded in 1652 after a split within the Accademia degli Immobili (Academy of the Immovables); after first being installed at the Teatro Cocomero, *Gli Infuocati* would transfer to the Teatro alla Pergola. Unfortunately, the entrance and this bomb are all you can see of the theatre at present, financial difficulties having forced Teatro Niccolini, which in the 1980s was home to Carlo Cecchi's *Granteatro*, to close its doors. The building, which is privately owned, has occasionally been used for such special events as receptions or fashion shows, but it seems that the dilapidated state in which it now finds itself can only get worse. If you ever get the chance, don't hesitate to visit the interior, where

a majestic staircase dominated by a huge mirror leads to a vast white auditorium adorned with stucco-work; there, the gently sloping stalls are surrounded by three ranks of boxes under a ceiling with a magnificent chandelier. The whole thing is now bathed in silence, the aftermath of a different sort of "bomb" to that depicted on the façade: the devastating effects of property speculation and inadequate funding for the arts.

WALLED-UP WINDOW IN PALAZZO PUCCI

33

Reminder of a failed assassination attempt against Cosimo I de' Medici

Via dei Pucci, at the corner of via dei Servi

In Florence as elsewhere there are numerous reasons for walling up a window. But that at the corner of Via dei Pucci and Via dei Servi was bricked up for a very special reason: to ward off evil and set an example. The window is on the ground floor of the palazzo of the Pucci family, traditional allies of the Medici. This connection had brought the Pucci various important public offices in Florence, but then, in 1560, Pandolfo de' Pucci was banished from the court of Cosimo I for immoral behaviour. He took the punishment so badly that he was soon planning an attempt on Grand Duke Cosimo's life, hiring two assassins to do the job. These murderers were expected to keep watch for the grand duke from this window in Palazzo Pucci, because Cosimo regularly passed by when going from his own palace to attend Mass in the basilica of the Santissima Annunziata. However, as at the time of the Pazzi conspiracy, the gods smiled on the Medici, with the plot being discovered even before the conspirators could carry it out. Both the assassins, Pandolfo himself and various members of other noble Florentine families (including some of the Ridolfi) who had joined the plot were all hanged from a window in Bargello prison. However, retaliation did not stop there: Cosimo, who it seems never entirely got over the conspiracy, ordered that Palazzo Pucci itself should be punished, by walling up the window from which the two killers were to have fired on him.

The grand duke thus achieved various goals. First, he did not have to change his route to the basilica of the Santissima Annunziata; every time he passed by here, he was reassured by the fact that the window was no longer a source of possible danger. Secondly, that condemned window stood as a manifest sign of his power and vengeance. Indeed, the humiliation inflicted on the very fabric of the Palazzo Pucci would outlive the Medici dynasty itself, for no one has ever dared to reopen the window.

Florence's finestrelle

Via del Corno, 3 - Borgo Santa Croce, 8 - Borgo San Frediano, 7r

Although easy to overlook, certain Florentine palaces have special little windows. These *finestrelle* ("little windows") were not intended just to allow light and air to enter corridors or storerooms but had a much more specific function: they were specially installed so that the children of the house could watch what was happening in the street without having to heave themselves up to a window-ledge from which they might fall. Set beneath the windows "for adults", these *finestrelle* were deliberately small and protected by a narrow mesh grille. You can see more than one example strolling around the streets of the old city centre, but if you want to be sure of finding one go to the back of Palazzo Vecchio, in Via del Corno; alongside Santa Croce, in Borgo Santa Croce (which is actually the building where Vasari had his studio); to the Borgo San Frediano in the Oltrarno district. By definition, these are mere details of Florentine architecture, but they reveal the care taken by architects and their clients when thinking about the needs of those who were going to live in the buildings.

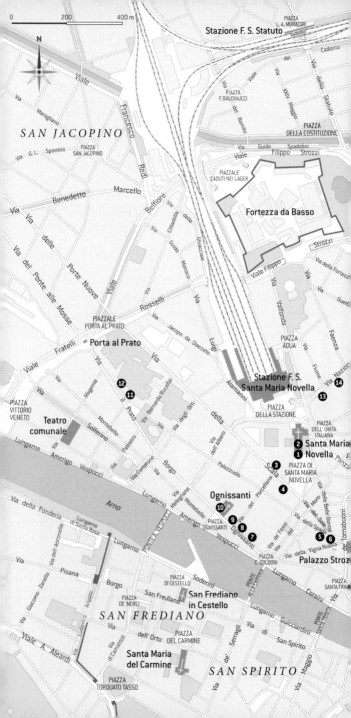

Santa Maria Novella

ARMILLARY SPHERE IN THE CHURCH OF SANTA MARIA NOVELLA

The sphere at the origin of the Gregorian calendar

Church of S. Maria Novella
Piazza di S. Maria Novella

Ignazio Danti, a Dominican monk who was also an astronomer and cartographer, included two astronomical instruments in the façade of the church of Santa Maria Novella. To the right of the entrance is a marble gnomon*, to the left a bronze armillary sphere (see below). It was with these instruments that Friar Danti calculated the discrepancy between the solar year and the Julian calendar, which had been devised by Julius Caesar in 46 BC, promulgated by law the following year and had

remained in force ever since. Having persuaded Pope Gregory XIII to recognise the importance of his calculations, the Dominican scholar then formed part of a committee of scientists (headed by Christophorus Calvius) which would successfully argue for the introduction of the new, "Gregorian", calendar. As already mentioned, the realignment involved skipping ahead ten days, passing directly from October 4 1582 to October 15 1582.

The Julian calendar

The Julian calendar, developed during the reign of Julius Caesar (hence the name), remained in force until the reform introduced by Pope Gregory XIII in 1582. The Gregorian calendar which takes its name from that pope introduced a reform in the counting of leap years, which had previously meant that the date indicated by the calendar fell further and further behind the solar date. The most spectacular effect of the introduction of the new calendar was, in fact, the suppression of ten days. And this is why St Theresa of Avila died on the night between October 4 and October 15 1582.

Ignazio Danti's work came to fruition in 2016, when the meridians on the church floor were finally completed. On 22 September each year, coinciding with the autumn solstice, you can observe the passage of two small discs of sunlight formed by rays passing through two holes: one in the stained-glass of the *Coronation of the Virgin* and the other in the façade. In fact, Danti had failed to complete his astronomical device because of disagreements with the new Grand Duke Francesco I de' Medici. But 441 years later, the accuracy of his calculations was confirmed.

Italy's first digital public clock

The pendulum on the façade of Santa Maria Novella railway station still uses the original mechanism dating back to 1935, making it the first digital public clock in Italy.

A gnomon is the upright on a sundial whose shadow is cast onto a flat surface.

Tornabuoni chapel's giraffe "camelopardo"

Santa Maria Novella church
Piazza di Santa Maria Novella
Open: weekdays from 9am to 5.30pm, Fridays 11am to 5.30pm, Saturdays 9am
to 5pm, Sundays and public holidays 1pm to 5pm

The Medici, in common with other aristocrats of the time, had no
hesitation in exhibiting exotic animals at public events or to enter-
tain important guests.

Even the Marzocco, a heraldic symbol of Florence and of the Roman
founding colonies, is a lion. As long as the Medici ran the city, several
lions were kept in a menagerie near the Palazzo Vecchio, still known as
Via dei Leoni (Street of the Lions), representing the power and strength
of Florence.

In 1487, a strange new animal came to enrich the Medici wildlife collection. Sultan Qaitbay of Egypt, on an official visit to the city, gave Lorenzo de' Medici a giraffe, described as "seven arms" high, with "feet like an ox" and so docile that it could harmlessly take an apple from a child's hand.

That wasn't the first time a giraffe had visited Florence – one had arrived in 1459, apparently for an exotic hunt. But this novelty aroused such curiosity among the citizens that the giraffe was exhibited several times in the streets before finally finding refuge in the cloister of a convent.

The latest giraffe's notoriety was such that Florentine Renaissance painter Ghirlandaio included it in his *Adoration of the Magi* in the Tornabuoni chapel of Santa Maria Novella (Andrea del Sarto did the same with his *Julius Caesar Receives Tribute* fresco in the Villa Medici at Poggio a Caiano, near Florence).

Sadly, the animal failed to adapt to Florence's harsh winter climate and died on January 2 1488.

MUSEUM OF THE OFFICINA PROFUMO-FARMACEUTICA OF SANTA MARIA NOVELLA

Museum of a temple to body care

Via della Scala, 16
Tel: 055 216276
Pharmacy open all year round (except Christmas and two weeks in mid-August) from 9.30am to 7.30pm
Visits, on request, to the pharmacy museum Monday–Friday between 10.30am and 5.30pm • For guided tours, book at visteofficina@smnovella.com
Admission free

The famous old pharmacy of Santa Maria Novella has a small and little-known museum that you can visit on request – an opportunity to see the sacristy frescoes by Mariotto di Nardo. The museum has a library of specialist books: ancient volumes of recipes for the preparation of medicaments, botanical treatises and also richly illustrated volumes that bring home how harmoniously the sciences were once linked with the fine arts. In the other rooms are collections of mortars, porcelain medicine jars and glass bottles of all sizes in which perfumes were mixed and preserved. There is also a curious collection of the apparatus for processing the herbs used in the preparation of essential oils. All these articles reflect a period in the history of pharmaceutical sciences; authentic works of art, their splendour is in keeping with this wonderful historic pharmacy, which is one of the oldest in the world and has been in business for centuries. First established in 1221 by the Dominican monks who had recently arrived in Florence, the pharmacy only began selling to the public in 1612. After a series of trials and tribulations in the nineteenth century – the refurbishment in a neoclassical style of certain rooms (for example, the one used for retail sales) and ultimate confiscation and nationalisation by the state in 1866 – the pharmacy was then sold into private ownership. The Officina has now transferred its production facilities to workshops in Via Reginaldo Giuliani. However, all its products are still made using traditional methods and natural oils, and bear such evocative names as *Alkermès*, *Acqua di Rosa*, *Elisir de Cina* and *Aceto dei Sette Ladri* (Seven Thieves Vinegar) – each of which sounds as if it could furnish the plot for an old and exotic movie.

NEARBY
The meeting of two saints ④
Loggiato delle Leopoldine
Piazza Santa Maria Novella

At the end of the great arcaded loggia of the Spedale delle Leopoldine (formerly Ospedale di San Paolo and now home of the Museo Novecento: Museum of the 20th Century) is a glazed polychrome terracotta lunette by Andrea della Robbia featuring two male characters embracing – none other than St Francis and St Dominic. According to tradition, the two saints met in the piazza (which was then outside the city walls) in 1221, the year of Dominic's death. They were apparently visiting their respective Orders, as the Dominicans already owned the church of Santa Maria Novella, and the Franciscans the Ospedale di San Paolo. Whether this is historically accurate or not apart from the historical veracity of this encounter, the lunette represented the seal of fellowship that prevailed between the two Orders.

REPRODUCTION OF THE HOLY SEPULCHRE IN JERUSALEM

Heart of Christian Jerusalem in Florence

Cappella Rucellai
Access via Museo Marino Marini
Piazza San Pancrazio
Open Saturday, Sunday, Monday from 10am to 7pm, Wednesday–Friday 10am to 1pm, closed Tuesdays and public holidays
www.museomarinomarini.it

This small chapel alongside the former church of San Pancrazio – which today houses the Museo Marini – contains a little-known reproduction of the Holy Sepulchre in Jerusalem. The Rucellai family had close links with the Middle East (their family crest was a galleon with billowing sails) and the Holy Land was the source of the plant, subsequently cultivated in the Oricellai Gardens, which was used to obtain violet dye for wool. These links with the holy places of Christianity were such that it was decided to reproduce within Florence the heart of the most important of all Christian sanctuaries: the Holy Sepulchre. While the atmosphere inside this chapel remains intimate and powerful, little trace of the solemnity within these old walls can be seen on the outside. The small doorway gives onto a narrow pavement in a street that has heavy through traffic, and it is from this inauspicious exterior that you enter a sanctuary of mystical harmony. The particular character of the interior owes a great deal to the architectural harmony of this small rectangular temple, which was completed by Leon Battista Alberti in 1467. The very proportions seem to be inspired by secret designs and an encoded language. The floor is a geometric carpet of marble, while the walls are covered with symbols and figures inspired by a happy blend of Florentine humanism and the art of the Middle East. The entablature is engraved with a passage from St Mark's Gospel, while the upper part of the structure is enclosed by lily-shaped crenels and, as to be expected, the fifteenth-century ceiling is decorated with frescoes. This place is so small that it seems like a miniature temple fitted within the outer "box" of the chapel. The whole place is imbued with a kind of timeless gravity, and the fact that it is only open a few hours a week adds to the impression of a hidden jewel.

The decoration of the small chapel has also inspired modern architects such as Alvar Aalto, who made use of this scheme in his interior designs.

WINE BARS IN THE STREET

It was forbidden to serve salted bread with wine to increase the customers' thirst

Via delle Belle Donne 2
Via del Giglio 2
Borgo Pinti 24, 26, 27
Via Isola delle Stinche 7r

Passing from Via Tornabuoni into the eloquently named Via delle Belle Donne (Street of Beautiful Women), you'll see, just above a closed window hatch, a plaque with a string of regulations on the consumption of wine.

This hatch is one of the best preserved of Florence's *buche da vino* (literally "wine holes") and is inscribed with the opening hours for

each day of the week and each season: during public holidays, the wine counter closed in the early afternoon and not in the evening, as it did on normal days.

If you keep your eyes peeled, you'll notice other such counters in the city centre. One is just a short walk away, in Piazza Strozzi, and another superb example is to be found at No. 2 Via del Giglio; there, the hatch is in the form of the doorway to a palazzo set within a miniature reproduction of the rustication that was so typical of numerous Florentine palaces. To the upper left of the doorway is a marble plaque that gives the wine counter's opening hours. These are slightly longer than those in Via delle Belle Donne, which is logical perhaps, given that the family that owned this palazzo had as its motto Per non dormire ("So as not to sleep"), which is actually engraved on their palazzo in Piazza Santa Trinità (see p. 35).

The hotel Monna Luisa at No. 27 Borgo Pinto also contains a *buchetta* within the foyer of the building (open to the public). Although the current owners have placed a large plant in front of the hatch, the opening with its two support ledges (for bottles) lets you see how these flourishing businesses actually worked.

The *buchetta* in Via Isole delle Stinche, on the other hand, is now associated with ice cream rather than wine: it graces the façade of the famous Vivoli ice-cream shop.

The boom in such wine counters began in the seventeenth century, when Florence's commercial fortunes had gone into decline. Such outlets allowed families who owned vineyards to make extra money by selling their produce directly to the public. The trade was strictly regulated by the authorities – for example, it was forbidden to serve salted bread with the wine to increase a customer's thirst – and the wine was sold in the sort of straw-covered bottles still seen today (the straw protected the bottles when they were brought in by cart from the countryside). These drinks counters (*mescite*) were so popular because you could buy wine directly in the street, without having to pay the mark-up charged in inns and taverns; and, of course, the wine producers themselves benefited because they had another outlet for their produce.

Sometimes people also left a small pot of wine and some crusts of bread on the ledges of these wine hatches, so that the city's paupers could help themselves anonymously.

There are also some *buchetta* outside Florence: in Volterra (No. 6 Via Buonparenti) and at Colle Val d'Elsa (No. 14 Via Campana). See *Secret Tuscany* in this series of guides.

BAPTIST CHURCH

Beatification of Stenterello

Borgo Ognissanti
Worship at 10.30am every Sunday

Open only once a week, on Sunday morning, the Baptist Church of Borgo Ognissanti, a short walk from Piazza Goldoni, is unusual in being a theatre converted into a place of worship (unlike so many churches and oratories in Florence that have done the opposite and become theatres after deconsecration). Here, the altar has in a way got its own back, the crucifix standing on the spot once occupied by a stage. These secular origins are no secret, and the Florence Baptist Church retains all the characteristics of a theatre interior. However, as a recent plaque records, this wasn't just any old theatre: it was the birthplace of the variety character Stenterello.

At the time the small theatre was known as the Teatro Ognissanti (or Teatro Solleciti), and it was here that Luigi del Buono invented this cunning but ingenuous character, whose trademarks were his lanky form and stockings that didn't match. The theatre itself was founded in 1778 and remained in business until 1887. A few years after its closure it was bought (in 1895) by the Baptist Church, then funded by the sizeable British community in Florence.

A recent plaque commemorates the foundation of the theatre, even if perhaps the most important date associated with it is February 16 1791, when Italy's first production of *Hamlet* was staged.

As in deconsecrated churches turned into theatres, here the original function of the building is clear, giving this church a rather theatrical air that makes it so much easier to conjure up the atmosphere of the performances at the Teatro Solleciti.

The first feature that immediately strikes you is the row of columns around the perimeter. These columns once supported the boxes and balcony, although now they support a sort of chancel. And if you look carefully at the polygonal apse, you can see how it echoes the form of an apron stage; in fact, the prompt box now leads to the baptismal fonts (in what used to be the actors' dressing rooms). The very place where Stenterello so often put on his costume and make-up is now where people are baptised! It's as if the Word of God had taken over where the tales of his adventures left off.

HOUSE OF GIOVANNI MICHELAZZI ⑧

Art Nouveau in Florence

Borgo Ognissanti, 26

A rt Nouveau – known as *Stile Liberty* in Italian – never enjoyed great success in Florence. Its sinuous, free-flowing forms and plant-motif decorations may have been considered an affront to the linear rigour and elegant sobriety of the traditional Florentine style. However, not far from Florence in Borgo San Lorenzo, the heart of the Mugello, the Chini family founded a dynasty that became famous for its Art Nouveau work. Whereas in numerous other European countries, Art Nouveau resulted in swelling curved balustrades, oval windows and asymmetrical doorways, the Chinis in Florence were rather more restrained, working in a place which would have ridiculed the more extreme trends then in fashion. Thanks to the architect Giovanni Michelazzi, there are at least some remarkable Art Nouveau buildings in Florence, beginning with No. 26 Borgo Ognissanti. A slim structure with large, very unusual windows flanked by stylised sculptures, this has a small main doorway that marks a felicitous break with traditional architectural canons. The numerous details may at first appear extravagant but they follow the criteria of a new code of aesthetics – and are certainly striking when seen in this street. Still, the Florentine bourgeoisie were clearly not great fans of such innovations, for the only other significant examples of Art Nouveau are outside the city centre: the building of the Galleria Carnielo in Piazza Savonarola and, above all, the Broggi-Carceni and Ravazzini villas at Nos. 99 and 101 Via Scipione Ammirato. Both villas are the work of Giovanni Michelazzi, with Villa Ravazzini decorated with ceramic tiles by Galileo Chini.

NEARBY

Palazzo Baldovinetti: the upside-down house   ⑨

Borgo Ognissanti 12

Not far from here – at No. 12 Borgo Ognissanti – stands the curious *casa alla rovescia* (upside-down house). Palazzo Baldovinetti owes its nickname to the rather original architectural design: when you stand on the opposite side of the street and look at its window balustrades, balcony and the large consoles supporting it, you'll see that they're all the wrong way round. By some architectural wizardry, the design overburdens the façade while at the same time making it special. It's said that this "reversal" of the usual order of things was because of the narrowness of the city streets – the construction of houses with balconies was banned (it's true that an old building complete with balcony is rarely seen here). However, Baldovinetti did everything he could to obtain a permit for a balcony, convinced that Borgo Ognissanti was wide enough. In the end (around 1530) Alessandro de' Medici gave in to yet another application, but with the words: "Go on, you can build your blasted balcony! But upside down!" – never imagining that the architect would be able to meet that challenge to the letter.

THE BOOK IN THE FRESCO OF
SAINT AUGUSTINE IN HIS STUDY

Botticelli's joke

Church of Ognissanti
Piazza Ognissanti
Open to the public: from 7.30am to 12 noon and from 4pm to 7pm, closed
Friday mornings and occasional afternoons

Florentines have always been great practical jokers, such as the great Brunelleschi in his *Novella del grasso legnaiuolo* (Story of the Fat Carpenter), or Machiavelli in his satirical play *La Mandragola* (The Mandrake). Even Renaissance master Sandro Botticelli subtly concealed a joke in one of his sacred paintings, which however has nothing funny about it. The fresco in the church of Ognissanti depicts St Augustine of Hippo wreathed in an air of inspired meditation, withdrawn in his study and surrounded by objects such as a mitre, an armillary sphere and a solar calendar. In an environment devoted to serious learning, what can the artist's joke be? Sharp-eyed visitors will notice that the open pages of the book above St Augustine's head are covered with scholarly illustrations of geometry and scribbled writing.

Only one line is really legible, and Botticelli has helpfully marked it with a small cross in the left margin. Reading this line is disconcerting: it says, *Dov'è Frate Martino? È scappato. E dov'è andato? È fuor dalla Porta al Pra-*

to (Where is Brother Martin? He fled. And where did he go? He left by the Porta al Prato.). Nobody is sure exactly what the artist was referring to, but everything points to a joke at the expense of one of the church brethren who was prone to unexplained absences.

Besides the tomb of Botticelli (1445–1510), Ognissanti is also the last resting place of actor Luigi Del Buono (1751–1832), who has a double plaque on his tombstone. One inscription was requested by Del Buono himself, asking for devotion to the Blessed Virgin; the other remembers the "playwright and creator of the Florentine character, Stenterello".

"GARAGE"
FOR *IL BRINDELLONE*

A wooden door of unusual size

Quartiere del Prato, alongside No. 48
The door can always be seen from outside
Open only once a year, on Easter Sunday
Other, rare, opportunities to visit are the so-called "Open Door" days organised
by the City Council (dates from City Hall information offices)

Strolling through the Prato district, there's nothing of particular note until you reach No. 48. There, the sharp-eyed will spot a huge yet narrow wooden wall that stands as tall as the two buildings either side of it. Closer inspection reveals a double door of quite extraordinary size: in fact, this is the entrance to the space for storing what Florentines affectionately refer to as *Il Brindellone*, the wagon that is used during Easter Sunday celebrations. Whereas everyone has heard of the *Scoppio del Carro* (Explosion of the Wagon) folk tradition that takes place on that day, most people are unaware of this "garage" – even if they have wondered what happens the rest of the year to this magnificently decorated three-tier wagon. The famous *scoppio* takes up the tradition of the "holy fire" which in the Middle Ages was lit by rubbing together the fragments from the Holy Sepulchre which Godfrey of Bouillon (a medieval Frankish knight, one of the leaders of the First Crusade) had given to Pazzino de' Pazzi, who had distinguished himself in the assault on the walls of Jerusalem during that Crusade. The tradition survived even the disgrace into which the Pazzi family fell after their unsuccessful plot against Lorenzo de' Medici and his brother Giuliano. Over time, the celebration developed to include the use of this enormous three-tier triumphal wagon, lined with fireworks to be lit by the columbina – a rocket in the form of a white dove.

The failure of the fireworks to ignite is seen as an omen of bad luck (for example, in 1966 – the year of the disastrous flood – that's what happened). The firework display lasts around twenty minutes in all and symbolises the flames of holy fire spreading around the city.

For the Easter celebration, *Il Brindellone* is drawn to the cathedral by two white cows; but for the rest of the year the enormous wagon is housed here. The historic procession begins as soon as the wagon leaves its sanctum, whence it is returned after being escorted around the city. Apart from a few exceptional occasions, Easter morning is the only chance to witness the complex operation involved in throwing open these huge doors concealed between the two buildings and wheeling out the triumphal wagon.

GIARDINO CORSINI AL PRATO

⑫

One of Italy's finest privately owned gardens

Via Il Prato, 58
Open all year: from 8am to 12.30pm and 2.30pm to 6.30pm (in winter, until
sunset); closed on Saturday afternoon and Sunday
Admission: e7; group concessions
To visit the garden when closed to the public, call 055 218994
www.artigiantoepalazzo.it

While the Prato district may have got its name from the term for meadow (*prato*), open expanses of grassland are a rarity here now. Still, the place does contain one of the finest privately owned gardens in Italy, concealed behind the walls of Palazzo Corsini. That garden is home to 130 tortoises, one for each of the lemon trees. And it is within that orchard that an exhibition entitled *Artigianato e Palazzo* (Craftwork and the Palazzo) is held every year in June. Devoted to the finest craftwork produced in Florence, this event offers food and wine tastings as well as practical demonstrations of such "minor arts" as decoration, bookbinding, locksmithery, marquetry, quality leatherwork and all the other trades in which ancient craft traditions are maintained and developed. The event is also one way for this garden and palazzo to keep abreast of the times – even if over the centuries they have already had to adapt to changing circumstances and tastes. When Bernardo Buontalenti designed the building in 1572, he envisaged a garden of geometrical paths outlined by hedges, with the greenery completing his own architectural designs. About fifty years later (in 1624), that geometrical layout was altered by the addition of various Baroque features designed by Gherardo Silvani. One of the special features of this garden is its central avenue flanked by statues of

decreasing size meant to create the illusion that the perspective runs much deeper than it actually does. In the eighteenth century, when one of the Corsini family became pope (Clement XII), the loggia was adorned with numerous plaques bearing inscriptions in Latin, Greek and even Etruscan. Around 1860, the garden underwent another substantial change, when it was adapted to meet Romantic canons of taste; on that occasion, for example, the old ragnaie (nets spread to catch insects) were replaced by two copses of tall trees. Today, with its avenue of Roman statues, Teatro di Verzura (an open-air theatre currently being restored), famous lemon trees and tortoises, this wonderful garden is a secret haven in the heart of the city.

LITTLE-KNOWN TREASURES OF THE FRATELLI ALINARI COMPANY

Art printworks, library and archives ...

Fratelli Alinari
Largo Fratelli Alinari, 15 • Tel. 055 23951
Stamperia d'Arte Alinari: visits on request by writing to negozio@alinari.it
Biblioteca Alinari: visits on request by writing to biblioteca@alinari.it
Archives consultable online at www.alinari.com or via fototeca@alinari.it

The location of Fratelli Alinari, not far from the Alinari National Museum of Photography in Piazza Santa Maria Novella, is no co-incidence, for these are the historic premises of the Alinari brothers photography workshop, a pioneer of its kind in Europe. Besides the offices and other administrative services, there are art printworks, a library and archives.

The printworks and the library are a continuation of the museum tour. In the former you can discover the wonders of collotype, an early procedure for reproducing photographic images on paper using a glass plate. The Alinari photography works is the only one in the world that still has the equipment – and, above all, the technical expertise – to carry out this work, using collotype to reproduce photographs and daguerreotypes; images of old or contemporary works of art, pictures of frescoes, paintings, sculpture and buildings; and two-colour drawings – all without the inevitable "hallmarks" of industrially produced images.

The library not only contains thousands of books on photography but also rare complete editions of the magazines that are themselves part of the history of this artistic discipline – for example, *Camera Work*, edited in New York by Alfred Stieglitz from 1903 to 1917, or the *Bollettino della Società Fotografica Italiana*, published in Florence from 1889 to 1912. The archives (which can be consulted online) contain four million images: the sum of the Alinari collections and of the collections put together by numerous other art or photographic historians. There are also 45 million photographs from archives in Italy or abroad that are represented (or administered) by the Fratelli Alinari company. Even though they have never left the largo (square) at the end of Via Nazionale which now bears their name, the Fratelli Alinari have clearly come some way since they first set up shop.

What is collotype?

This technique consists in coating a glass plate with a special layer of dichromated gelatine and then drying it carefully in an oven for a few hours. The negative is then applied to this plate, which is immediately inked by hand and then pressed onto paper using a hand press. The care needed for each phase of this process is so meticulous that a collotype plate produces only a limited number of reproductions – 500 at most; any more and the layer of gelatine is damaged. Each numbered collotype image is thus one of a limited series.

FRESCOES IN GARAGE NAZIONALE

"Automobile" frescoes in an art garage

Via Nazionale, 21
Tel: 055 284041
Open: from 6am to midnight Monday–Saturday; 7am to 1pm and 3pm to 10pm Sundays and public holidays
Charges vary, according to type of vehicle, from €23 to €33 per day or €3.70 to €5.20 per hour

The car park in Via Nazionale is worth a stop, if only for an hour, partly because it is like no other garage in the city, partly because it is in a street that is always crowded with traffic.

In 1987 the Garage Nazionale decided to enliven the daily life of the city's motorists by commissioning Carlo Capanni to paint two remarkable frescoes of vintage and modern Italian cars alongside the access ramps.

Along with filling stations decorated with ceramics, this is yet another example of how art can be applied in an everyday context – a modern expression of that great Florentine tradition of beauty "accessible to all".

Stavini, a contraction of sta fra i vini

Stavini - Viale Fratelli Rosselli 22-26 rosso • Telefono: 055 211488

In business since 1940, this motorcycle parts shop in Piazza Ognissanti is special because of the name of the owner: Roberto Stavini, whose own father, Amadeo, was the first and only person in Italy with this surname. A contraction of *sta fra i vini* (he lives among wines), the name was chosen by the Corsini family of San Piero a Sieve for an abandoned child they brought up. The family were in fact dedicated to viticulture and the production of wine, and this foundling became their chauffeur. Perhaps it is this association with motor vehicles that led his own son, Roberto, to open a motorcycle parts shop.

Designer to the pumps

Piazza Donatello – Piazza Ferrucci

Nothing could be more anonymous than a filling station. Florence, however, has succeeded in enlivening some of them – even if passing motorists rarely pay attention to the results. No one knows who was the first to suggest decorating them with ceramic tiles. Whoever it was, the idea has borne fruit and motorists can now refresh their aesthetic sense at these three garages:

Agip in Piazza Donatello;

Esso in Piazza Donatello;

Api in Piazza Ferrucci.

In the two Piazza Donatello stations, the walls facing the traffic have been decorated with pictorial ceramics; the tiles in the Agip station are even signed (*B. Lucchesi*).

The inspiration for the decoration is the two themes of travel and fuel. You can, for example, see St Christopher (the patron saint of travellers) and an oil well alongside an avenue bordered with trees and various monuments; other features include a petrol lamp and the famous Agip symbol of a six-legged dog spitting fire. A short distance away, the Mobil-Esso station is decorated with a single vast image in ceramic tiles depicting the union of water and sky, complete with fishes and birds, sun and moon. The signature is hieroglyphic, with the date 1954.

In Piazza Ferrucci, the elegant modern filling station in red brick is decorated on various sides with Florentine themes rendered in contemporary ceramics, all signed *Mario Dal Mas Fecit* 1961.

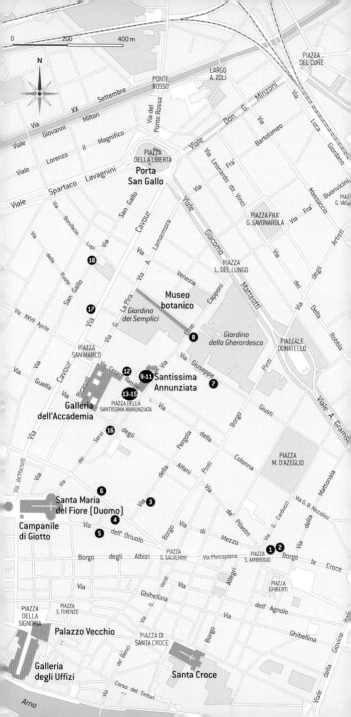

SS Annunziata

TABERNACOLO DEL MIRACOLO DEL SANGUE

*Where the feast of Corpus Domini originated:
the Sant'Ambrogio Miracles*

Church of Sant'Ambrogio
Piazza Sant'Ambrogio
Open daily: from 8am to 12 noon and 4pm to 7pm

To the left of the high altar in the church of Sant'Ambrogio (St. Ambrose) is a chapel that commemorates the miracle which took place here on December 30 1230, when the surrounding area was still countryside. Also mentioned in the *Chronicles* of Giovanni Villani, the story goes that the parish priest, Ugoccione (or Uguccione), discovered

a few drops of blood within the chalice he had used in celebrating mass. He declared it a miracle, a claim which was sanctioned by the bishop after a day of strict observation.

It was this event – together with another of the same kind which took place a little later in Bolsena – that would lead to the institution of the Feast of Corpus Domini in 1264.

The miraculous blood of 1230 was regularly carried in ritual procession, and over a century later – in 1340 – it would cause another miracle, which spared Florence from the plague. In 1595, there was yet another miraculous escape. When a fire broke out around the altar, the flames reached the tabernacle where the ciborium was kept but did not damage the consecrated hosts; indeed, when the water used to quench the fire touched the hosts, they took on a circular form and were thereafter kept as holy relics.

Over time, Sant'Ambrogio was adorned with various art works recounting these miracles. In the fifteenth century, the relics were transferred from the high altar to the chapel on the left; the marble tabernacle is the work of Mino da Fiesole and shows Uguccione handing over the blood he had discovered to the Mother Superior of the nuns attached to the church. As for the second miracle, it is depicted in a fresco by Cosimo Rosselli showing the procession in Piazzetta de Sant'Ambrogio (which serves as the church parvis). The artist included a self-portrait amongst the crowd of worshippers.

NEARBY
Blazon of The "Red City" ②

Another curiosity at Sant'Ambrogio can be seen upon leaving the church. On the outer pier at the corner of the façade is a small blazon of the "red city" (*Città Rossa*), and at the corner of Via de' Macci are sixteenth-century plaques referring to "The Great Monarch of the Red City" (also mentioning the tabernacle of Sant'Ambrogio). These were the heraldic devices of a local student confraternity founded at Sant'Ambrogio in the fourteenth century.

TELETROFONO OF TEATRO DELLA PERGOLA

The world's first telephone

Via della Pergola, 12–32
For times of guided tours, in Italian and English, call 055 2264364
http://www.teatrodellapergola.com/

Teatro della Pergola is the oldest theatre in Italy, with an oval auditorium for acoustic effect and tiered boxes. Not only is the leading light of "Italian" theatres still working, but the stage hides a little gem of technology: the "teletrofono", the world's first telephone, developed by Antonio Meucci (1808–1889) while he worked at La Pergola as a technician. Meucci invented this novel voice communication system so he could quietly tell the technicians in the flies when to lower scenery to the stage.

On the stage itself is a plaque commemorating this device, which Meucci perfected when he left to work in the United States. He set up a private telephone line from his New York theatre so he could speak to his sick wife at home. Thus the telephone was born through an act of love.

La Pergola contains other little-known wonders that can only be discovered on a guided tour: below the stalls, the complex mechanism that allowed the area to be raised to stage level to create a single large ballroom; a small museum below the auditorium where various memorabilia are displayed; the specialist library; a section of the street dating back to the eighteenth century and lined with artisans' workshops, which has been swallowed up in the space next to the stage; the small nineteenth-century salon and the sumptuous neoclassical foyer; a well and some basins for washing and dyeing costumes; and the legendary "primo camerino" (principal dressing room) built directly on stage for one of the greatest actors of all time, Eleonora Duse. Among these wonders you'll discover not only stucco, canvases and bas-reliefs but several commemorative plaques: besides Meucci's, others are dedicated to Eleonora Duse and theatre practitioner Gordon Craig, Verdi's Macbeth, and theatre director Orazio Costa, who set up a training centre whose last home was the Pergola. There are two ways you can visit this theatre: the classic "guided" tour; or "discovery trails" where you can "meet" along the way some of the historical figures who have contributed to La Pergola's fame.

Who really invented the telephone?

Until 1989, no one had ever questioned that it was Alexander Graham Bell who invented the telephone. But then Basilio Catania, former director-general of CSELT (the Italian telecommunications research and development agency), discovered the work that Antonio Meucci had done as a theatre technician in Florence. According to Catania, the Telettrofono voice communication system developed in 1850 would have allowed Meucci to communicate between his office and his invalid wife's room, paralysed as she was by osteoarthritis. Ten years later, Meucci is said to have given a demonstration to his friend Enrico Bendelari, an experiment that was described by a New York-based Italian-language newspaper, *L'Eco d'Italia*. Again according to Catania, it was in 1874, when Meucci contacted the Western Union Telegraph Company for a demonstration, that the despoliation began. During the next two years, Meucci was never able to carry out his demonstration and ended up losing the rights to his invention in 1876, lacking the means to renew his patent. It was also during these two years that Bell is thought to have stolen Meucci's invention, Catania claims, as Bell must have worked in the laboratory where Meucci kept his devices.

Bell filed his telephone patent in March 1876. According to Catania, a commission of inquiry revealed a secret link between patent office employees and Bell's company, which had undertaken to transfer the rights to 20 per cent of his invention to the Western Union.

JOURNEY AROUND ROMAN FLORENCE

Florentia: the last remnants of a ghost city that still makes its presence felt

Guided tours first Sunday of each month
Tours begin at the Firenze com'era museum in Via dell'Oriuolo, 24
Tour times: 10am – 11.30am, 11am – 12.30pm and 12 noon to 1.30pm
Tel: 055 2768224

Some of the Florence that was known as *Florentia* still survives; now hidden and underground, these remnants sometimes re-emerge, sometimes call upon us to rediscover them. On the first Sunday of each month, Florence City Council organises a tour around Roman Florence, which begins with a clear and instructive lecture in the rooms of the Firenze com'era (Florence as it was) museum in Via dell'Oriuolo, where a model of the Roman *Florence* shows it to be much larger and more magnificent than you might have thought. This combination of visual illustrations and commentary gives a real idea of the urban development of Roman Florentia, locating its boundaries and main buildings in relation to the present-day urban fabric. But then you move on from models to the real thing, leaving the museum to walk to Piazza San Giovanni, where there was a city gateway with the rather splendid name of Porta contra Aquilonem (Gate against the North Wind). The tour continues along Via Roma (the *cardus* – that is, the north-south axis – of the Roman city) to what was the heart of Roman Florence: the present-day Piazza della Repubblica, which was once the site of an imposing temple to Jupiter, Minerva and Juno, of which no trace survives. A little farther on

– between Via del Proconsolo and Piazza San Firenze – work is still ongoing at the archaeological site around the ancient temple of Isis which was first uncovered at the end of the eighteenth century. Recent finds here include various tombs (other remains of Roman Florence to be seen in the Torre della Pagliuzza museum at the Hotel Brunelleschi, in Piazza Elisabetta). Nearby, the cellars of the restaurant Alle Murate also contain remains of Roman buildings, and the tour ends in the cellars of Palazzo Vecchio, where excavations have revealed fragments of a Roman theatre.

"The Stendhal Syndrome is no aesthetic ecstasy but rather the result of a tilted head restricting blood flow"

When visiting Florence, *Homo turisticus* has so much to see that he feels he must carry on relentlessly. As soon as he arrives by train or plane, he finds himself immersed in a cultural heritage whose wealth has no equal in the world; wherever he goes in the city centre, art is on his heels, reminding him of his duty. And forced into contemplation, he ends up having hallucinations: too much beauty, too much happiness, too many emotions – all these go to reinforce the sense of displacement resulting from the loss of habitual points of reference and continual encounters with the sublime. This can produce a certain malaise, a sudden need to rest and drink something. And in the worst cases, one ends up not in a street-side café but in an ambulance, suffering from more extreme symptoms: dizziness, heart flutters, black-outs. These are the classic symptoms of what for the past thirty years or so has been referred to as the "Stendhal Syndrome", and the hospital of Santa Maria Nuova has a department that specialises in this psychosomatic affliction suffered by over-enthusiastic tourists. The name comes from the fact that Henri Beyle, better known as Stendhal, records suffering from just such symptoms when, in 1817, he visited the church of Santa Croce to see the tombs of Michelangelo, Galileo and Alfieri, as well as the ceiling frescoes by Volterrano. In his *Rome, Naples et Florence*, he writes: "I was already in a sort of ecstasy at the mere idea of being in Florence... Absorbed in the contemplation of sublime beauty, I saw beauty close-to; I might be said to be touching it. I had got into that state of feeling in which the celestial sensations resulting from the fine arts overlap with the passions. Upon coming out of Santa Croce, my heart was pounding... I walked as if I were afraid of falling over." These symptoms have been known to affect travellers to other cities – in particular, Jerusalem and Paris: in one due to the overwhelming religious presence of the place, in the other due to the rhythm and majesty of the urban fabric. But it would seem that in Florence the sole cause is beauty alone. For certain physicians, the "Stendhal Syndrome" has a much more prosaic explanation: it is due to the circulatory problems caused by continually holding the head tilted to look up at cupolas, bell-towers and frescoes. The admiration of beauty, it seems, stops an adequate flow of blood to the brain.

Annals and archives

Palazzo Bastogi Bastoni
Via dell'Oriuolo, 33
Tel 0552616527
Free admission upon prior booking at archstor@comune.fi.it
Visits must be at the following times: Monday and Friday 9am to 3.30pm and
Tuesday, Wednesday and Thursday 9am to 6pm

The historical archives of Florence are an inexhaustible mine of wealth, a labyrinth of documents where a story leads to another. You could spend one's whole life here without ever getting bored – or perhaps just fifteen minutes or so relaxing in a most unusual and educational manner. There are not many cities where the historical archives are so readily accessible, and also house interesting temporary exhibitions. Located in Via dell'Oriuolo, the archives occupy rather narrow premises opposite the former Oblate Convent now the City Library. There are tens of thousands of documents, all divided into different collections. The material covers all aspects of social life in the city, from dossiers on the bodies involved in public assistance and the proceedings of the City Council, to records of the financial and artistic affairs of the Teatro Niccolini (1699–1932) or documents regarding the four-century-long history of the Ospedale di San Giovanni di Dio (1604–1968). Each of these collections casts new light on a specific aspect of the city's history – ranging from the fairly brief period when Napoleonic Florence was governed by a French-style *mairie* to the records of the Scuole Leopoldine, where the individual histories of the pupils illustrate the position of women in the worlds of work and education over a period of around two centuries. As for the collections of drawings, these comprise some 40,000 documents that date from the period ranging from the end of the eighteenth century to the 1960s. There are, for example, the plans relating to the rebuilding of Florence after the Second World War, with various unpublished architectural designs. Along with any temporary exhibitions being held, don't miss out on visiting the elegant study room, which is open to the public. This is a pleasant place to spend half a day searching through the documents and chronicles that record the "everyday" history of the city.

An army of 1,500 model soldiers

Exhibition space of Cassa di Risparmio di Firenze
Via Maurizio Bufalini, 6
Open: Monday–Friday from 9am to 7pm, Saturday and Sunday from 10am to 1pm and 3pm to 7pm
Tel: 055 5384001
Admission free

One thousand five hundred lead soldiers illustrating the Napoleonic wars and part of the Italian Risorgimento: Alberto Predieri (1921–2001), president of the Florentine savings bank, amassed a treasure trove that he bequeathed to the bank. Since then, the institution has set up a small museum so that everyone can enjoy this marvellous collection.

The lead soldiers are all carefully painted, many are unique pieces, and most are 54 millimetres tall. With their authentic uniforms, finely detailed armaments and flags, and expressive rather than simply "ceremonial" poses, this collection represents all the main Italian and European armies. The Russian horsemen of the Starinski regiment, the Royal Scots Greys cavalry charging on the battlefield of Waterloo, the Austrian riflemen, the Mamelukes of Napoleon's Imperial Guard, the Genoa cavalry of the Kingdom of Sardinia, and so on.

There are numerous historical figures, from the inevitable Garibaldi, Napoleon and Frederick II of Prussia to the kings of Sweden and Naples. The collection includes a number of extras such as coaches, mobile canteens and supply wagons – not to mention military bands, mess rooms, sentry boxes, artillery – representing almost every aspect of army life.

One of the most moving scenes is a reconstruction of the Napoleonic retreat from the frozen wastes of Russia, a three-dimensional drama with some soldiers dying in the snow and others painfully dragging their remaining equipment past the corpses of men and horses. The chronologically organised exhibition, with succinct historical captions and maps, gives an overview of European wars from the end of the eighteenth to the beginning of the nineteenth century. A unique display that cannot fail to move you, even if you're not particularly keen on lead soldiers.

The preposterous façade of the German Art Institute

Kunsthistorisches Institut
Via Giusti, 44

Located between Piazza D'Azeglio and Piazza Santissima Annunziata is a palazzo unique in Florence - a spectacular demonstration of how aesthetic canons can change. During the Renaissance no-one would ever have thought of creating so eclectic and idiosyncratic a façade for a palazzo, but by the end of the sixteenth century adherence to the rules was obviously much less strict. The Mannerist painter Federico Zuccari did not stay in Florence a long time, though he did paint the huge (recently restored) fresco of *The Last Judgement* in the cupola of the Duomo. For some time, he lived not far from here – in Via Capponi, next-door to the house occupied by Andrea del Sarto (whose residence here is now commemorated by a plaque). However, Zuccari then decided to build himself a home, in a Mannerist style that would be a public affirmation of his personality as an artist. Thus, in the years 1578/79 he created this house, with a façade that is more like a pastiche than a composition, as its various components are organised in a very theatrical manner: panels of bare brick and blocks of unfinished rock alternated with polished blocks of stone, bas-reliefs depicting the symbols of Painting, Architecture and Sculpture (re-worked in 1920), windows with opulently decorated gratings, two niches, stone benches at pavement level and a cartouche (now covered with roughcast) which Zuccari was to have adorned with a fresco. This whole façade is the frontage to a tall narrow building that appears even more incongruous compared to the other structures in this quiet street. If Zuccari aimed to leave some unusual and indelible record of his passage through Florence, then he certainly succeeded. Today, the Palazzo Zuccari houses the Kunsthistorisches Institut. At present Florence's most influential foreign-run institute for art history studies, it has one of the best specialised libraries on this subject – with more than 300,000 books and a thousand or so specialist magazines that would be difficult to find elsewhere. There is also an immense collection of photographs of Italian art. A highly esteemed centre of research, this institute has been in existence since the end of the nineteenth century, its academic rigour in a sense counterbalanced by the sheer exuberance of Zuccari's façade.

Zuccari was also responsible for another eccentric house, this time in Rome, in Piazza di Spagna. That structure has windows in the form of large open mouths, giving the impression of monstrous gaping jaws. (See our *Secret Rome*.)

PALAZZO CAPPONI ALL'ANNUNZIATA

A small hidden palazzo

Via Gino Capponi, 26
Open: first Monday of the month from 3pm to 6pm, advance booking required
at 329 7066422

Some distance from the city's main palazzi, the eighteenth-century residence commissioned by the Marchese Alessandro Capponi (who died before the construction work was finished) is located in a long, narrow street that makes it difficult to appreciate the vast façade. Nevertheless the imposing building is full of surprises and has hosted illustrious guests, notably poet Giuseppe Giusti, who died there in 1850, and statesman Gino Capponi. It also houses one of the first Italian collections of Cézanne's paintings. Some features resemble Palazzo Pitti on a smaller scale, such as the central section flanked by two wings, the large inner courtyard, and the fountain like a shell-covered grotto. And Palazzo Capponi also has a park extending behind the building, a geometrically laid-out garden adjoining that of the Gherardesca, with a good view of the imposing rear façade.

There's also one rather odd building, a long pavilion with a dozen arcades designed to house aviaries and glasshouses filled with lemon trees, decorated with mosaics, statues and obelisks. The first thing that strikes you inside the palazzo is the sumptuous nymphaeum covered with inlaid shells and the spectacular staircase in *pietra serena* (grey sandstone), rising towards the ceiling frescoed with an allegory of Triumph.

Going from one room to another, each painted with magnificent frescoes, including the great banqueting hall with its interior balcony, you'll see countless neoclassical statues and meticulous decorative details – mirrors, door handles, fireplaces – all signs of great wealth.

Palazzo Capponi is an obvious contrast to Palazzo Uguccioni (see p. 55) on Piazza della Signoria: from the outside it almost seems to hide discreetly away, in spite of its vast dimensions, without revealing the splendour inside.

CLOISTER OF THE DEAD

A secluded cloister in the church of the painters

Church of La Santisssima Annunziata
Piazza Santissima Annunziata
Open: from 7am to 1pm and 4pm to 7pm • Considering when Masses are
celebrated, it is better to visit the church between 4pm and 5pm
To reach the Cloister of the Dead, go to the far end of the church; the entrance is
on the left behind a red curtain

Y ou can end your tour to the architectural complex of La Santissima Annunziata by visiting a little known part of the church: the
Cloister of the Dead, which is reached from the side aisle on the left.
This secluded part of the monastery not only contains numerous tomb-
stones but also – above the doorway into the church – a magnificent
Madonna del Sacco by Andrea del Sarto and a cycle of eighteenth-century frescoes depicting various scenes in the history of the Servites (*I
Servi di Maria*). The other side of the cloister gives access to the Chapel
of the Company of Saint Luke, the confraternity of Florentine painters
and the precursor of the Accademia delle Arti e del Disegno created by
Cosimo I. In effect, this – the most important Marian sanctuary in the
whole of Florence – would during the course of the sixteenth century be the workplace of such great artists as Andrea del Sarto, Pontormo, Rosso Fiorentino, Luca Giordano, Bronzino, Perugino, Vasari and
many others (including artists from Flanders and Germany). Within
the Santissima Annunziata, these artists would paint religious scenes or
specific episodes of religious life, their activities here being reflected in
the legend surrounding the image of the Virgin by Frà Bartolomeo (see
double page overleaf). Certain artists – for example, Baccio Bandinelli,
the Flemish artist Jan van der Straet and the Frenchman Giambologna
– are buried here; Domenico Passignano actually painted his own tomb
within the monastery. Amongst the figures which appear in *The Coming
of the Magi* in the Ex-Voto Cloister are a self-portrait of Andrea del Sarto
and a portrait of his friend Jacopo Sansovino.

Deliberate damage to a painting

One part of the painting entitled *The Marriage of the Virgin* is
damaged.
This mutilation is said to be due to the artist himself, Franciabigio,
who was angered by the fact the monks were always looking over
his shoulder as he worked.

The two tabernacoli *in the centre of Arco San Pierino, Via dell'Oriuolo*

Inside the arch in Via dell'Oriuolo is an elegant niche that stands
empty, with no hint of an image. On the arch itself, on the other
hand, a small polychrome Madonna is embedded in the wall, without a frame. A few metres apart, the niche without an image and the
image without a frame seem complementary, like the two halves of
one of those small street tabernacles.

FRA BARTOLOMEO'S PAINTING OF THE VIRGIN

A rare acheiropoieton

Church of La Santissima Annunziata
Piazza Santissima Annunziata
Open: from 7am to 1pm and 4pm to 7pm • Considering when Masses are celebrated, it is better to visit the church between 4pm and 5pm

The church of La Santissima Annunziata (The Blessed Virgin Annunciate) contains a painting that is the object of a famous legend: Fra Bartolomeo's Virgin. During the period of the first religious foundation here, around 1252, this monk (not the famous one of the sixteenth century) was said to have fallen asleep whilst completing the face of the Virgin in a painting, and when he woke up he found the picture finished; however, the actual painting dates from the fourteenth century and was partially repainted in the fifteenth. Such images are referred to as *acheiropoieta* (see opposite). It is perhaps a unique example of such a religious image in Florence. In this particular case, the *acheiropoieton* could be said to confirm the very special link there has always been between the church of La Santissima Annunziata and the art of painting.

Acheiropoietic *works of art*

In the Christian tradition, the term *acheiropoieton* refers to works of art "not made by the hand of man". Thus it relates to images created either by transposition from direct contact (as with the Shroud of Turin and the Veil of Veronica) or by divine intervention. This term was apparently coined by St Paul himself in a particular context: during a stay at Ephesus, he rose up against pagan idolatry and especially against the numerous many-breasted statues of Artemis, mother of the gods. He declared that the "gods made by the hand of man are not gods". With the use of this term *acheiropoieton* he showed respect for the Judaic prohibition of images, attacked pagan idols by setting the actual body of Christ against them, and limited eventual abuse by also claiming that this body of Christ was exclusively in the form it took after the Transfiguration, in other words after an event that followed the Resurrection. Besides the celebrated Shroud of Turin and the Veil of Veronica (see Secret Rome in this series of guides), tradition holds that a few other rare acheiropoietic images still exist today. One example is to be found at Mount Athos in Greece: this theocratic monarchy, isolated on a peninsula in north-eastern Greece since the eleventh century and out of bounds to women, children and female animals, is home to two *acheiropoietic* icons. One is in the monastery of the Great Lavra and the other in the monastery of Iviron.

In France, there is also an acheiropoieton in the church of Notre-Dame-des-Miracles at Saint-Maur near Paris (see our guide *Banlieue de Paris Insolite et Secrète*, not yet available in English). Similarly, the Holy Visage of Edessa, now in the Bartholomite Church of Genoa, is said to have been painted by Christ himself. The painting of Christ in the Sancta Santorum of the Lateran in Rome is said to have been drawn by St Luke and then completed by angels, and the famous sculpture of the Holy Visage in Lucca (Tuscany) is said to have been

started by Nicodemus (who, together with Joseph of Arimathea, was present at Christ's crucifixion), but then completed by angels (see our guide *Secret Tuscany*). In Venice (see our *Secret Venice*), the chapel of Saint Lucy in the church of Santi Geremia e Lucia contains a miraculous sculpture of Christ which was inexplicably "completed" after the death of the Capuchin friar who had begun the work and yet had never been able to model the face to his satisfaction.

PRIVATE CORRIDORS OF PRINCESS MARIA MADDALENA DE' MEDICI

A princess who didn't want to leave the house

Via della Colonna, via Laura, via Capponi
Basilica of Santissima Annunziata

Eighth child of Ferdinando I de' Medici and Christina of Lorraine, sister of Cosimo II, Maria Maddalena de' Medici (1600–1663) suffered from a congenital deformity that prevented her from walking unaided. She was not baptised until the age of 9. On May 24 1621 she entered the Convento della Crocetta (Convent of the Little Cross), but never took her monastic vows. She lived in the palazzo next to the Crocetta (the work of architect Giulio Parigi), in the block between No. 38 Via della Colonna, Piazza Santissima Annunziata, No. 13 Via Gino Capponi, No. 15 Via Laura and No. 65 Via della Pergola. The site, which is now the headquarters of the Museo Archeologico Nazionale di Firenze (National Archaeological Museum of Florence), includes some older houses overlooking Via della Pergola. As the princess had great difficulty climbing stairs, her rooms were connected by a series of raised corridors through which she could move around easily and, above all, avoid crossing the street and attracting attention. Some intriguing traces of these corridors can still be seen today. In the palazzo itself (now converted into a museum), a long elevated corridor is known as the *corridoio mediceo* (Medici corridor) after the Vasari corridor, the elevated enclosed passageway built in 1564 by Giorgio Vasari to link the Uffizi with Palazzo Pitti. Maria Maddalena used hers to move about unobserved on the first floor. Two corridors overlooking Via Laura took her to the convent, and from there to the nearby monastery of Santa Maria degli Angiolini, which lay between Via Laura, Via della Pergola and Via della Colonna. Another corridor in Via della Colonna leads to what is now the Istituto degli Innocenti (Institute of the Innocents), and a final one overlooking Via Gino Capponi let her attend Mass in the basilica of Santissima Annunziata. Above the main door of the church you can still see a large barred window, from which the princess could follow the service without being seen.

ISTITUTO GEOGRAFICO MILITARE ⑫

Headquarters of Italian cartography

Via Cesare Battisti, 10
Admission by appointment Monday -Friday from 9am to 1pm
Tel: 055 2732244

A simple phone appointment will allow you to visit a place which is set within the old city centre and yet is itself an entire world – indeed, universe. Concealed between Piazza San Marco and Piazza della Santissima Annunziata, the Istituto Geografico Militare is a true national treasure, set up here when Florence was capital of the Kingdom of Italy (from 1865 to 1870). Indeed, one of the first tasks undertaken by the new institute was the production of the first topographical map of a united Italy; to a scale of 1:100,000, this was an immense project that took more than thirty years' work to complete. The institute is fascinating not only for those with a

passionate interest in cartography, but also for those who are merely curious about antique planispheres and atlases; the wonderful examples here have been housed in the magnificent rooms of this seventeenth-century palazzo for almost 150 years now. The collection also contains 200,000 books and a substantial body of photographic material, as well as geographical, chorographical, hydrological and geological maps of Italy, Europe and the entire world. The large salon, which used to be the meeting-place of a famous cenacle, is magnificently decorated with seventeenth-century frescoes and lined on two sides with monumental bookcases; the space in the middle of the room is occupied with various globes. Whilst housing a historic library and museum of cartography, the place is also a fully functional scientific institution, whose task is to constantly update cartography on the basis of the scientific instruments available. The military personnel are friendly and helpful; and whilst the silence of these vast rooms reveals that they attract few visitors, you somehow get the impression that the whole of the world is gathered there.

THE BEES ON THE EQUESTRIAN MONUMENT OF FERDINANDO I

A symbol of power become a game for children

Piazza Santissima Annunziata

This must be the most stylised depiction of insects in the whole world. Indeed, at first glance it is difficult to identify this motif on the bronze pedestal of the equestrian monument to Ferdinand I de' Medici, grand duke of Tuscany from 1587 to 1609. Designed by the Mannerist sculptor Giambologna but actually cast by his pupil Pietro Tacca (in 1608), the statue was made from the bronze cannons on Turkish ships seized by the Order of the Knights of Santo Stefano. On examing at the plinth, you'll see what at first sight looks like a circle dotted with balls; however, this is not just a circular decorative motif but a swarm of bees, surmounted by the significant inscription *Maiestate Tantum* (meaning that for Ferdinando to govern "his Majesty sufficed").

These insects are intended as a symbol of power, to be read in various ways. Not only do they refer to the state as a community, as a place of industry and disciplined organisation, but also to the "queen bee's" supremacy over the whole (a symbol of the authority of the grand duke).

Such an unusual depiction of a swarm of bees has spawned urban legends. Both children and adults play the game of trying to count all the individual bees. But it is said that, after a certain number, you inevitably lose count because of the irregular concentric arrangement of the swarm. This little puzzler was perhaps intended, both the grand duke and Tacca wanting to illustrate to the populace that they were incapable of grasping the full sense of supreme power.

It is said that parents nowadays use this swarm to test their children's power of concentration, rewarding them if they manage to count up the exact number of bees. It is also said that if you do count them – without touching or pointing – then you will enjoy good luck.

For those who do not want to take this opportunity to put themselves to the test, the answer is that there are 91 bees. But does that total include the queen bee or not?

THE "BABY HATCH"

From 1445 to 1875

Ospedale degli Innocenti
Piazza della Santissima Annunziata

This Ospedale degli Innocenti is famous for its museum (which contains various fine works of art), for the fact that it houses the UNICEF Innocenti Research Centre concerned with children's rights, and for one very special historic artefact: its famous "foundings wheel", where families – or single mothers unable to raise their child – abandoned unwanted infants.

This apparatus made it possible to commit this desperate act anonymously without leaving the child to die. It took the form of a sort of "baby hatch", located under the arcades to the left of the hospital entrance. Alongside was a string attached to a bell used to attract attention, so that the abandoned infant would not be left out in the open air for too long. The rotating cylinder is no longer extant, but the hatch itself has not changed since February 5 1445, when it received its first "innocent", a girl who was named Agata after the saint whose feast day was celebrated on that date. The system itself was not abolished until 1875, some time after the unification of Italy and Florence's period as capital of the kingdom. A plaque now commemorates its use. However, the orphanage of the Innocenti was not always the final destination of these abandoned infants. When they had been gathered in from the "wheel", they were sent to the Loggia del Bi-

gallo, near the Duomo, where they were put on public display, hoping either that they would be adopted or that their repentant parent(s) would come back and claim them.

What is most striking nowadays is the actual beauty of the foundling wheel, which gives the impression of being a fine example of the applied arts rather than an instrument of social assistance. The Florentines affectionately refer to it as *la mangiatoia* (the manger), a term which conjures up thoughts of Christmas and the nursery. The truth is that the word here designates a mechanism that was far from cosy, yet did mark an advance in levels of social assistance.

The foundlings' wheel

It is said that in 787, Dateus, a priest in Milan, began placing a large basket outside his church so that abandoned infants could be left there. More organised initiatives for the reception of abandoned children were begun by the Hospice des Chanoines in Marseilles from 1188 onwards, with Pope Innocent III (1198–1216) later giving the practice the Church's benediction; he had been horrified by the terrible sight of the bodies of abandoned infants floating in the Tiber and was determined to do something to save them.

So the doors of convents were equipped with a sort of rotating cradle which made it possible for parents to leave their children anonymously and without exposing them to the elements. The infant was left in the outside section of the cradle, and then the parent rang a bell so that the nuns could activate the mechanism and bring the child inside. Access to the "turntable" was, however, protected by a grille so narrow that only newborn infants would fit through...

Pope Gregory VII, Genghis Khan and Jean-Jacques Rousseau are some of the famous personalities who were abandoned as babies.

Little used during the nineteenth century, the system had to be readopted after some twenty years at various places in Europe due to the sharp upturn in the number of infants abandoned.

Foundlings' wheels of historical significance can be seen at the Vatican and in Pisa and Florence (see *Secret Tuscany* and *Secret Rome* in this series of guides), Bayonne (France) and Barcelona (see *Secret Barcelona*).

THE OPEN WINDOW
IN PALAZZO GRIFONI

A haunted room?

Piazza della Santissima Annunziata

T is is one of the enigmas of Florence: the second-floor window on the left-hand side of the façade of Palazzo Grifoni is said to be "always open", its shutters ajar.

The story goes that it was from here that a member of the Grifoni family bid farewell to her husband as he set off for war. Thereafter, she languished at the window, waiting in vain for his return. When she herself died, it was decided to finally close the window. But then, some say, the room seemed to become haunted: paintings came away from the walls, lights went out for no apparent cause and furniture mysteriously shifted from one place to another. Once the window was re-opened, everything went back to normal.

Other sources have it that local residents demanded that the window stay open because they had become so used to seeing it like that.

Whatever the truth, those half-open shutters can have a strange effect upon the passers-by who cross Piazza Santissima Annunziata every day, suggesting that one the "Mystery of the Open Window" has yet to be resolved.

NEARBY
Garden of Palazzo Grifoni – Budini Gattai ⑯
Via dei Servi, 51
Open: second Wednesday of the month from 9am to 12 noon and 2.30pm to 5.30pm, except in August, by appointment at 055 210832
Discover more about the palazzo's history by visiting the garden, famous for its collection of centuries-old camellias and its nymphaeum. Inside you can see Bartolomeo Ammannati's vestibule with its monumental staircase. But the room with the legendary window is closed to the public ...

MONKEY AT CASINO MEDICEO DI SAN MARCO

A symbol of curiosity?

Via Cavour, 57
Closed to the public

At No. 57 Via Cavour, going from Piazza San Marco towards Piazza della Libertà, you'll find the Casino Mediceo di San Marco, former property of the Medici family. The palazzo's austere façade is enlivened by some rather eccentric details. For example, above the wooden doorway and below a window a carved monkey's head and hands seem to be crushed by a large shell suspended over them.

Some people interpret the monkey figure as a representation of the essence of evil while the shell symbolizes fertility and life – evil being overcome by good. It's also claimed that the monkey epitomizes curiosity. Undoubtedly no coincidence as this was the site of the alchemical experiments of Grand Duke Francesco I de' Medici (1541–1587), a man constantly motivated by the thirst for learning.

The monkey could also indicate the passage from the inanimate to the animate, a transformation often evoked in the research of medieval alchemists (see page 15).

A plaque on a high wall next to the palazzo commemorates a Florentine institution that has now disappeared but is still very interesting in artistic and historical terms. This was the medicinal gardens of San Marco, a vast country estate where Lorenzo de' Medici set up a court academy of the arts under the direction of Bertoldo di Giovanni. It was frequented by artists such as the young Michelangelo. The plaque also mentions that the Accademia degli Orti Medicei was the first of its kind in Europe.

In 1576, the site was partly taken over by the Casino Mediceo, commissioned by Francesco I as his laboratory, passionate as he was about the natural sciences and chemical experimentation. It was known as the Fonderia (Foundry). Francesco never lived there, however, and at his death bequeathed it to his son by his mistress Bianca Cappello, Don Antonio de' Medici (1576–1621). In 1597, the palazzo became Don Antonio's official residence and he embellished the rooms and gardens with sculptures by Giambologna.

PALAZZO PANDOLFINI

A building originally designed by Raphael

Via San Gallo, 74
Open: every last Monday and Saturday of the month, by appointment, from
10am to 1pm, closed in August
Tel: 338 7229862 (10am to 12.30pm and 6pm to 8pm)

Seen from the street, Palazzo Pandolfini seems curiously laid out: a main building with two storeys (unlike the traditional three), next to a single-storey wing with an entrance gate overlooked by a series of balconies. Despite features such as rustication, the tympana above the windows, and even the stone balustrades supported by short columns, it doesn't look anything like a Florentine palazzo. Another difference is the strange inscription running around the ledge below the roof of the main building, bearing the names of its patron Bishop Giannozzo Pandolfini and of the Medici popes Leo X and Clement VII. The palazzo also lacks the traditional stone bench

at street level, although the design of the window balustrades seems to hint at this. This unusual complex is the result of a series of incidents during the construction work. Raphael had conceived the project in 1514, but as he couldn't leave Rome because of St Peter's, he delegated Palazzo Pandolfini to his faithful colleague, Giovan Francesco da Sangallo. The work was next interrupted by the death of Giannozzo Pandolfini and the appointment of his heir, Ferrando, Bishop of Troia, in Puglia, and then by the long siege of Florence, during which Sangallo died (1530). He was eventually succeeded by another architect from the Sangallo family, Bastiano, known as Aristotile for his air of sententious gravity. In the meantime, however, the overall vision had been compromised and the palazzo was left unfinished, yet retained a curious charm thanks to its myriad and harmoniously arranged details.

Behind the building is a garden once noted for its collection of camellias and cineraria and a glasshouse devoted exclusively to orchids, a series of mythologically themed statues and a splendid galleried orangery.

The tour includes the former Oratorio di San Silvestro, which has been incorporated into the house beyond the great monumental staircase.

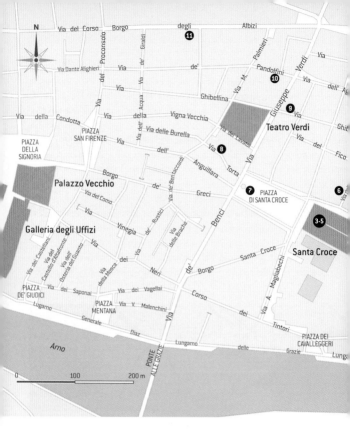

Santa Croce

FLOOD MARKERS

An "Arnometer"

Via Ghibellina, corner of Via delle Casine
Via de' Neri, corner of Via San Remigio

A first glance there's nothing special about the corner of Via Ghibellina and Via delle Casine. But on moving a little closer to the building there, you'll find something that reflects an aspect of the city's history: markers of the levels reached by the Arno floodwaters on various occasions. About 1 metre above ground level is the inscription *1547 – ARNO FU QUI AL 13 AGOSTO* (1547 – Arno reached here on August 13), with a line indicating the high-water mark five centuries ago. That particular flood was all the more extraordinary because, unlike the others, it happened at the height of summer. Slightly higher up is a bronze plaque commemorating the disastrous flood of 1844, and then – much higher up (more than 4 metres above ground level) – is the third plaque which reads *IL 4 NOVEMBRE 1966 L'ACQUA D'ARNO ARRIVÒ A QUEST'ALTEZZA* (On 4 November 1966 the waters of the Arno reached this height). What we have here could perhaps be described as an "Arnometer", measuring the behaviour of the river in exceptional circumstances. On the corner of Via San Remigio and Via de' Neri are two other inscriptions, recalling exceptional floods more than six hundred years apart. Higher up – at 4.92 metres above ground level – is a plaque that indicates the level reached by the floodwaters of the Arno on November 4 1966, while just below is another marker which refers to the year 1333 and bears the inscription "during the night of Friday 4 November the waters reached here". Yes, quite incredibly, the two monstrous floods happened on the same date! Apart from those two floods, the worst were those of 1466, 1547 and 1844. None, however, match up to that of 1966, which killed thirty-four people, left 100,000 Florentines trapped

on rooftops or in the upper storeys of buildings for a full day and night, swept away 15,000 cars and caused untold damage to the city's art treasures. A torrent of mud, for example, swept into the church of Ognissanti and damaged Botticelli's fresco of *St Augustine*; the magnificent tombs in the church of Santa Croce were buried under 4.5 metres of slime; in the Uffizi the floodwaters reached the third floor. However, miraculously, all the city's bridges withstood the flood.

WINDOW WHERE ELIDE BENEDETTI MET HER TRAGIC END ②

"The city's most moving tragedy"

Via San Giuseppe, opposite the eponymous church

Opposite the parish church of San Giuseppe a recent plaque commemorates one of the most moving tragedies in Florentine history. Rather than the inscription, it is the window bars that attract attention, for it was here that Elide Benedetti, the most unfortunate of all the flood victims, died on November 4 1966.

Elide was 66 years old and confined to a wheelchair. By the time rescuers reached her the water was too high to bring her out through the doorway. Some *carabinieri* therefore raised her in a sheet tied to the window, to keep her above ground level while they went for help – and for something to cut the bars from the outside.

The parish priest, Father Giuseppe Baretti, stayed with the poor woman at the window, offering comfort as the situation became more and more dramatic. The flood waters, however, continued their inexorable rise, help did not arrive and Elide was drowned; Father Baretti found his courage failed him and he couldn't stay with her right to the end. A quote from the priest's diary is included on the plaque: "It was the most moving tragedy in the whole city. Assisting helpless while a woman who must die sees death approaching, and solely because we couldn't get through the window bars".

The plaque was raised by the parishes of San Giuseppe and Sant'Ambrogio in 2006, on the fortieth anniversary of the flood.

And if you're amazed that it took so long for such a public act of commemoration, you'll be even more so to learn that it took years to obtain the official number of victims. It was only recently that the Associazione Firenze Promuove managed to publish a Police Headquarters document dated November 1966, which gives a total of thirty-four people – seventeen in Florence and seventeen in the surrounding towns – listing the names of each and the circumstances of their death.

Peregrinations of Dante's monument: a very Florentine way of honouring the author of The Divine Comedy

Monuments to Dante in the Basilica of Santa Croce
Piazza Santa Croce and the Uffizi Loggia

When Santa Croce was finally consecrated as the mausoleum for the nation's famous sons, a large monument was erected for the tomb of the great Florentine poet Dante Alighieri. However, that tomb is now only a memorial, for Ravenna refused to give up the body of the poet whom Florence had condemned to exile. Anxious to make amends to this favourite son – and perhaps feeling a little guilty about the treatment he had received – Florence then honoured him with various gestures that were not always well thought out. For example, Via Dante may well be where the Alighieri family home once stood but it is just a minor side street – and the Casa di Dante museum is just a reconstruction. As for the most visible monument to the poet – the one in Piazza Santa Croce – that was initially a monumental gaffe: at first it was raised in the very centre of the square but then, not without some embarrassment, had to be moved to the left of the church's main doorway so as to allow cameras to film the games of "historic football" played here (see p. 204). The statue of Dante in Santa Croce shows the poet seated and leaning forward; the one in front of the church shows him standing with his right arm dangling at his side and his left wrapped in his gown; in the Uffizi Loggia, he is again shown standing but with his arm raised and his index finger near his nose.

The Florentine delight in earthy wit has seized upon the chance to ridicule these rather unfortunate poses, coming up with the observation: "In the church Dante's having a dump, in the square he's wiping himself and in the loggia he's sniffing his finger" – a dictum mentioned by the early-twentieth-century poet Venturino Camaiti, who wrote parodies of all 100 cantos of *La Divina Commedia*. Sharp-eyed visitors can decide for themselves if this brief description of the three statues is accurate. They might also ponder whether Ravenna, which boasts of having received Dante in the way he deserved, actually measures up to all these gestures of respect with which Florence the Incorrigible still commemorates its great poet. Perhaps the irreverence, though, is a form of popular affection, an expression of the fellow-feeling between the city and its most famous son. The familiarity may not be subtle, but it is undeniably a measure of the poet's prestige.

FAÇADE OF THE BASILICA DI SANTA CROCE

Star of David on a Roman Catholic church

Piazza Santa Croce

Until the nineteenth century, the façade of Santa Croce (Basilica of the Holy Cross) was left in undressed pietra forte (sandstone). The neo-Gothic design seen today was the work of the Ancona-born architect Niccolò Matas, who included in his designs a sign that bears witness to his own religious creed: the Star of David on the tympanum. Matas was also the architect of the monumental Porte Sante cemetery; however, for his own burial place he chose a plot directly opposite the main entrance to the basilica. This story has a curious antecedent in that, in the fifteenth century, the Franciscan monks of Santa Croce had rejected the designs by the architect Pollaiolo precisely because he wanted to include the family symbol of his patrons, the Quaratesi.

For more information about star of David, see next page.

The star hexagram: a magical talisman?

The hexagram – also known as the Star of David or the Shield of David – comprises two interlaced equilateral triangles, one pointing upwards and the other downwards. It symbolises the combination of man's spiritual and human nature. The six points correspond to the six directions in space (north, south, east and west, together with zenith and nadir) and also refer to the complete universal cycle of the six days of Creation (the seventh day being when the Creator rested). Hence, the hexagram became the symbol of the macrocosm (its six angles of 60° totalling 360°) and of the union between mankind and its creator. If, as laid down in the Old Testament (*Deuteronomy* 6:4–9), the hexagram (*mezuzah* in Hebrew) is often placed at the entrance to a Jewish home, it was also adopted as an amulet by Christians and Muslims. So it is far from being an exclusively Jewish symbol.

In both the Koran (38:32 et seq.) and *The Thousand and One Nights*, it is described as an indestructible talisman that affords God's blessing and offers total protection against the spirits of the natural world, the djinns. The hexagram also often appears in the windows and pediments of Christian churches, as a symbolic reference to the universal soul. In this case, that soul is represented by Christ – or, sometimes, by the pair of Christ (upright triangle) and the Virgin (inverted triangle); the result of the interlacing of the two is God the Father Almighty. The hexagram is also found in the mediated form of a lamp with six branches or a six-section rose window. Although present in the synagogue of Capernaum (third century AD), the hexagram does not really make its appearance in rabbinical literature until 1148 – in the *Eshkol Hakofer* written by the Karaite* scholar Judah Ben Elijah. In Chapter 242 its mystical and apotropaic (evil-averting) qualities are described, with the actual words then often being engraved on amulets: "And the names of the seven angels were written on the *mazuzah* … The Everlasting will protect you and this symbol called the Shield of David contains, at the end of the *mezuzah*, the written name of all the angels."

In the thirteenth century the hexagram also became an attribute of one of the seven magic names of Metatron, the angel of the divine presence associated with the archangel Michael (head of the heavenly host and the closest to God the Father). The identification of Judaism with the Star of David began in the Middle Ages. In 1354 King Karel IV of Bohemia granted the Jewish community of Prague the privilege of putting the symbol on their banner. The Jews embroidered a gold star on a red background to form a standard that became known as the Flag of King David (*Maghen David*) and was adopted as the official symbol of Jewish synagogues. By the nineteenth century, the symbol had spread throughout the Jewish community. Jewish mysticism has it that the origin of the hexagram was directly linked with the flowers that adorn the menorah**: irises with six petals.

For those who believe this origin, the hexagram came directly from the hands of the God of Israel, the six-petal iris not only reassembling the Star of David in general form but also being associated with the people of Israel in the *Song of Songs*. As well as offering protection, the hexagram was believed to have magical powers. This reputation originates in the famous *Clavicula Salomonis* (Key of Solomon), a grimoire (textbook of magic) attributed to Solomon himself but, in all likelihood, produced during the Middle Ages. The anonymous texts probably came from one of the numerous Jewish schools of the Kabbalah that then existed in Europe, for the work is clearly inspired by the teachings of the Talmud and the Jewish faith. The *Clavicula* contains a collection of thirty-six pentacles (themselves symbols rich in magic and esoteric significance) which were intended to enable communication between the physical world and the different levels of the soul. There are various versions of the text, in numerous translations, and the content varies between them. However, most of the surviving texts date from the sixteenth and seventeenth centuries – although there is a Greek translation dating from the fifteenth.

In Tibet and India, the Buddhists and Hindus read this universal symbol of the hexagram in terms of the Creator and his Creation, while the Brahmins hold it to be the symbol of the god Vishnu. Originally, the two triangles were in green (upright triangle) and red (inverted triangle). Subsequently, these colours became black and white, the

former representing the spirit, the latter the material world. For the Hindus, the upright triangle is associated with Shiva, Vishnu and Brahma (corresponding to the Christian God the Father, Son and Holy Ghost). The Son (Vishnu) can be seen to always occupy the middle position, being the intercessor between things divine and things earthly.

* qara'im *or* bnei mikra*: "he who follows the Scriptures". Karaism is a branch of Judaism that defends the sole authority of the Hebrew Scripture as the source of divine revelation, thus repudiating oral tradition.*
***Menorah – the multibranched candelabra used in the rituals of Judaism. The arms of the seven-branched menorah, one of the oldest symbols of the Jewish faith, represent the seven archangels before the Throne of God: Michael, Gabriel, Samuel, Raphael, Zadkiel, Anael and Kassiel.*

"HERMETIC" SKY OF THE PAZZI CHAPEL

The same night sky as San Lorenzo sacristy

Basilica di Santa Croce • Piazza Santa Croce
www.santacroceopera.it
Open: Monday–Saturday from 9.30am to 5.30pm; Sunday and Holy Days
of Obligation (January 6, August 15, November 1, December 8) 1pm to 5pm;
open Easter Monday, April 25, May 1 and June 2; closed January 1, Easter
Sunday, June 13, October 4 and Christmas Day • Admission: €5 (full price);
€3 (concessions); families: parents €5, children free

The frescoed cupola in the Pazzi Chapel alongside Santa Croce is painted with exactly the same star-studded sky as appears in the old sacristy of San Lorenzo (see pag. 127). This is unique: two frescoes commissioned from two different artists by two different patrons in two different parts of the city, yet both depicting the same – very significant – night sky.

Like the Medici, the Pazzi family maintained close relations with René of Anjou, the titular "King of Jerusalem", who during his stay in the city knighted one of the Pazzis and was present at the baptism of a child recently born to these aristocratic Florentines.

Hermes Trismegistus and Hermetism: attracting celestial energy to Earth by reproducing the cosmic order

Hermes Trismegistus, which in Latin means "thrice-great Hermes", is the name given by the neo-Platonists, alchemists, and hermetists to the Egyptian god Thot, Hermes to the Greeks. In the Old Testament, he is also identified with the patriarch Enoch. In their respective cultures, all three were considered to be the creators of phonetic writing, theurgical magic, and messianic prophetism. Thot was connected to the lunar cycles whose phases expressed the harmony of the universe. Egyptian writings refer to him as "twice great" because he was the god of the Word and of Wisdom. In the syncretic atmosphere of the Roman Empire, the epithet of the Egyptian god Thot was given to the Greek god Hermes, but this time was "thrice great" (*trismegistus*) for the Word, Wisdom and his duty as Messenger of all the gods of Elysium or Olympus.

The Romans associated him with Mercury, the planet that mediates between the Earth and the Sun, which is a function that Kabbalistic Jews called *Metraton*, the "perpendicular measure between the Earth and the Sun". In Hellenic Egypt, Hermes was the "scribe and messenger of the gods" and was believed to be the author of a collection of sacred texts, called hermetic, that contained teachings about art, science, religion and philosophy – the *Corpus Hermeticum* – the objective of which was the deification of humanity through knowledge of God. These texts, which were probably written by a group belonging to the Hermetic School of ancient Egypt, thus express the knowledge accumulated over time by attributing it to the god of Wisdom, who is in all points similar to the Hindu god Ganesh. The *Corpus Hermeticum*, which probably dates from the first to the third centuries AD, represented the source of inspiration of hermetic and neo-Platonic thought during the Renaissance. Even

though Swiss scholar Casaubon had apparently proved the contrary in the seventeenth century, people continued to believe that the text dated back to Egyptian antiquity before Moses and that it announced the coming of Christianity. According to Clement of Alexandria, it contained forty-two books divided into six volumes. The first treated the education of priests; the second, the rites of the temple; the third, geology, geography, botany and agriculture; the fourth, astronomy and astrology, mathematics and architecture; the fifth contained hymns to the glory of the gods and a guide of political action for kings; the sixth was a medical text. It is generally believed that Hermes Trismegistus invented a card game full of esoteric symbols, of which the first twenty-two were made of blades of gold and the fifty-six others of blades of silver – the *tarot* or "Book of Thot". Hermes is also attributed with writing the *Book of the Dead* or "Book of the Exit towards the Light," as well as the famous alchemy text *The Emerald Table*, works that had a strong influence on the alchemy and magic practised in medieval Europe. In medieval Europe, especially between the fifth and fourteenth centuries, hermetism was also a School of Hermeneutics that interpreted certain poems of antiquity and various enigmatic myths and works of art as allegorical treaties of alchemy or hermetic science. For this reason, the term hermetism still designates the esoteric nature of a text, work, word or action, in that they possess an occult meaning that requires a hermeneutic, or in other words a philosophical science, to correctly interpret the hidden meaning of the object of study. Hermetic principles were adopted and applied by the Roman *Colegium Fabrorum*, associations of the architects of civil, military and religious constructions. This knowledge was transmitted in the twelfth century to the Christian Builder-Monks, the builders of the grand Roman and Gothic edifices of Europe, who executed their work according to the principles of sacred architecture, true to the model of sacred geometry. It is the direct legacy of volumes three and four of the *Corpus Hermeticum*, according to which cities and buildings were constructed in interrelation with specific planets and constellations, so that the design of the Heavens could be reproduced on Earth, thus favouring cosmic or sidereal energies. All of this was done with the purpose of achieving the hermetic principle that states: "Everything above is like everything below". During the European Renaissance (sixteenth and seventeenth centuries), hermetism was replaced by humanism. Forms were rationalised and the transcendental ignored.

It was the end of the traditional society and the beginning of a profane, Baroque and pre-modernist society, paving the way for the arrival of the materialism and atheism that dominates the modern world. There were, however, some exceptions to this predominant rule in Europe. In Portugal, in the sixteenth century, the Master Builders, the heirs of the Builder-Monks, founded the Manueline style according to the hermetic rules of sacred architecture.

TOMB OF GIOVANNI BATTISTA NICCOLINI

Statue of Liberty – from Santa Croce to New York

Basilica of Santa Croce
Open: Monday–Saturday from 9.30am to 5pm, Sundays and public holidays
2pm to 5pm

Anumber of models are thought to have inspired the gigantic statue of *Liberty Enlightening the World* by young French sculptor Frédéric-Auguste Bartholdi, which France presented to the city of New York in 1886. First in line is the artist's mother, whose face is thought to resemble that of the statue; or it might have been Camillo Pacetti's so-called statue of the *New Law*, which stands on the balcony overlooking the main porch of Milan Cathedral (see *Secret Milan* in this series of guidebooks); or it may even have been the famous painting by Delacroix, *Liberty Leading the People*. So there's no lack of European echoes of the Statue of Liberty, including the 11 metre-high version erected on the Île aux Cygnes near the Pont de Grenelle in Paris, three years after the inauguration of the original in New York. The basilica of Santa Croce, with its huge collection of funereal monuments (around 300), likes to think it possesses one of the most reliable of all these plausible models.

The monument that Pio Fedi made for the tomb of Giovanni Battista Niccolini (1782–1861), nineteenth-century playwright and patriot, undeniably resembles the Statue of Liberty. It's not just the name of the memorial, *La Libertà de la poesia* (Liberty of Poetry), which suggests the resemblance, but the proportions between the parts of the body, the pose of the raised right arm, the gaze, the feet, and the crown with its projecting rays. The main differences are the broken chain in the hand of Pio Fedi's *Liberty*, instead of the torch brandished by Bartholdi's; and the more graceful air of the Santa Croce figure compared with the almost masculine or androgynous features of its "American sister". The Santa Croce monument was completed in 1877 and inaugurated in 1883, three years before the New York colossus. Designs for the statue had circulated among the artists of the time in the form of preparatory drawings, and a plaster model identical to

the finished work already existed when Bartholdi visited Florence. The French sculptor also had a strong connection with the Italian Risorgimento, one of whose poets was Niccolini. He often wore the red shirt of Garibaldi's soldiers and was an aide-de-camp, as well as a Freemason like the "Hero of Two Worlds" (as Garibaldi was known), as was Pio Fedi himself. So apart from the objective resemblance of the two works, the historical context seems to confirm the direct inspiration hypothesis.

PALAZZO BARGELLINI

Among the mayor's mementoes of the flood

Via delle Pinzochere, 3
Visits by appointment
Tel: 055 241724

Just a stone's throw from Piazza Santa Croce is the home of Piero Bargellini: Palazzo da Cepparello, dating from the sixteenth century, built in a style close to that of Giuliano da Sangallo and Baccio d'Agnolo. Piero Bargellini (1897–1980), writer and historian, deputy in the Italian parliament, and mayor of Florence at the time of the 1966 flood, acquired this palazzo in 1946 as a base for his many activities. His offices are in two large rooms with high coffered ceilings, decorated with half a dozen fourteenth-century frescoes from the church of Santo Stefano alle Busche in Poggio alla Malva – itself well worth a visit. In this residence, everything strikingly evokes Bargellini's work and human presence, such as the two pianos still played by his grandson, the famous pianist Gregorio Nardi, who (with his wife) is now the curator. Then there is the library, with its tens of thousands of letters, and a vast collection of books on the history of Florence. Bargellini was one of the first historians to systematically study certain local features such as the city's tabernacoli (street tabernacles) and place names. Several curious mementoes are also on display, such as the bag carried by the future mayor's wife during their Corsican honeymoon in 1929, when they travelled on foot and stayed with local people. The young couple were so emaciated on their return that their families made them take a month's cure at a specialist clinic. Bargellini's simple and sober personality is reflected above all in his extensive correspondence. Besides testimonies of friendship with the personalities who regularly visited his home, such as René Clair, Roberto Rossellini, Carla Fracci and Jean Gabin, there are innumerable letters from Florentines who approached the mayor to ask all sorts of favours, ranging from safeguarding the city's artistic heritage (the Historical Associ-

ation of Friends of Museums started life here) to help with personal matters. In their letters, some referred to agreements "made in tram No. 14" (Bargellini used public transport) or begged for money to meet their daily expenses, especially after the great flood of 1966, when the mayor asked his fellow citizens to write directly to him to circumvent bureaucratic delays. Every detail in Via delle Pinzochere brings to life not only the great humanity of the intellectual who lived there, but also the Florentine society of his time.

MARKINGS FOR A "FLORENTINE FOOTBALL" PITCH

Traces of the sport of yesteryear

Palazzo degli Antellesi
Piazza Santa Croce 20 and piazza Santa Croce

Played in period costume, *calcio storico* (literally, "historic football") is one of the curiosities of Florence. And that it is "historic" is evident in Piazza Santa Croce, where there are authentic traces of the Renaissance: the end markers of the halfway line across the pitch where the matches used to be played. The first of these markers is a marble disk set within the façade of Palazzo degli Antellesi, which stands to the left of a jewellery shop (on the right-hand side of the piazza as you look towards the church).

The date "10 February 1565" is carved in the stone. Directly opposite, on the façade of the building at No. 7, is the second marker. This smaller disk depicts a ball and is divided into four quarters: two red and two white. Before matches, a white line was traced across the square from the centre of one disk to the other; this marked the halfway line of the pitch where the two teams competed. At the centre of that line the *pallaio* (ball holder) would throw the ball into play by hurling it against one of the two disks; when it bounced back onto the pitch, the game had started. The matches were, however, sometimes played elsewhere: for example, in 1491 and 1605 they were held on the frozen surface of the Arno.

In 1530, when papal forces were besieging Florence, the city decided to show its contempt for the threat by sticking to their Carnival calendar,

despite the shortage of food. Thus the traditional match of *calcio fioren-tino* took place right under the eyes of the besiegers, camped on the hills around Florence. Unsportingly, the enemy even fired a cannon ball during play, which was greeted with vociferous booing from the Florentines. In 1575, Florentine merchants in the French city of Lyon decided to organise a match of *calcio fiorentino* – an event commemorated during the 1998 World Cup by a match between Florence and Lyon. It is even said that the development of the modern game in England is due to the fact that, in 1766, the English Consul witnessed a match of *calcio storico* played in Livorno. The famous players of *calcio fiorentino* included several members of the de' Medici family, as well as three future popes: Clement VII, Leo XI and Urban XIII (the latter was even born at No. 5 Piazza Santa Croce). The game, however, lost popularity in the seventeenth century, with the last known match being played in 1739.

Then, in 1930, the first match of modern times was played – to commemorate the 400th anniversary of the papal siege. Nowadays, a tour-nament is held every June between teams representing the four historic districts of Florence; the two elimination rounds and the final are played on a sand-covered Piazza Santa Croce. Often considered the ancestor of modern football, *calcio storico fiorentino* might just as readily be compared with rugby, given its rules and the robust physical contact that forms part of the game. Each match lasts fifty minutes and is played on a sand-covered pitch. For the modern tournament, the twenty-seven players are dressed in white (Santo Spirito), red (Santa Maria Novella), green (San Giovanni) and blue (Santa Croce). Once chosen from among the local nobility, the players representing the four districts these days are simply powerful – and ruthless – young men: the fact that you play (or used to play) *calcio storico* is a boast, a sign that you're tough, someone not to mess with. Even if the basic aim is to get the ball in the other team's net – and the game is not exactly "no holds barred" – this is a violent sport, and the games commonly end as they used to: in a general punch-up. All this is in stark contrast to the traditional cos-tumes worn by the players, which are often in shreds by the end of a game.

The name of the game may suggest some sort of pageant, but people still remember one match in which a player's ear was bitten off.

Some of the rough stuff is even politically motivated, at times requiring the police to intervene; in fact, for a few years the matches in Santa Croce were banned.

STROLLING ROUND THE EDGE OF FLORENCE'S FORMER AMPHITHEATRE

Imagine you can hear the crowds

Via Torta
Piazza Peruzzi

Near Piazza Santa Croce you can enjoy a stroll around an ancient monument that's no longer there. Perhaps disappointing for the tourist in search of spectacular ruins, this walk involves following an unusual curved line along these historic streets, where it takes an effort of the imagination to conjure up a vision of what once stood here.

The line follows the route of Via Torta (which, as a plaque notes, used to bear the significant name of Via Torcicoda (Tail Twister), Via del Parlascio (a *parlascio* or *parlagio* was a medieval term for a place of public assembly) and Via Bentaccordi round to Piazza Peruzzi. These streets form a loop unique in Florence, where roads are usually at right angles to each other. The curve reflects the semicircular outline of the old Roman amphitheatre; built in the

second century AD, it could hold up to 20,000 people (Rome Coliseum held up to 80,000) and had an arena of 64 metres by 40. The location was marshy land, as revealed by a number of surviving street names – Via Isole delle Stinche, Via dell'Acqua, Via Anguillara (*anguilla* = eel) – or even the name of the church of San Jacopo tra i Fossi (St Jacopo between the Ditches) that stands in nearby Via dei Benci. As for the name Via Burella, between Via Torta and Via dell'Acqua, it comes from the *burii* of the old amphitheatre, the underground passageways leading to the arenas.

The arch of the doorway at No. 6 Piazza Peruzzi corresponds to the longitudinal axis of the coliseum, and some houses in this street have rooms arranged in a sort of open-fan layout, indicating that they were built using the stones – or perhaps even a stretch – of the old amphitheatre, of which they form the sole surviving trace. The stroll certainly gives an idea of the size of the ancient amphitheatre and of how it was incorporated within the fabric of the developing city.

The Roman amphitheatre of Florence was where St Minias (San Miniato) was martyred. Tradition has it that, in AD 250, the Christian was beheaded in front of a jubilant crowd. However, the decapitated saint then stood erect, picked up his head and, holding it under his arm, walked proudly out of the arena. He then walked quickly to the Arno, crossed the river and went up the hill nearest the city centre. Once at the summit, he fell to the ground – exhausted by his ordeal or overwhelmed by the view. The Basilica di San Miniato al Monte was later built here in his honour.

The miraculous response of St Minias to decapitation recalls that of St Denis, Bishop of Paris (see *Secret Paris* in this series of guides). The phenomenon even has a precise name: *cephalophoria*, from the Greek *kephale* (head) and *phorein* (to carry).

PALAZZO BORGHESE

Nineteenth-century extravaganza

Via Ghibellina, 110
Visits require a few days' prior booking and depend on staff availability
info@palazzoborghese.it
Tel: 055 2396293
www.palazzoborghese.it

Even though a little cramped in the narrow Via Ghibellina, Palazzo Borghese stands out for its ground floor of undressed stone surmounted by a *piano nobile* (first floor) of neoclassical columns. This exterior gives no idea of the neoclassical opulence within, which does however strike you the moment you step into the entrance hall, where large Egyptian-style statues seem to stand in attendance. A little further on and you come to more statues, more columns and a monumental staircase. These form the core of an architectural composition within which are set mirrors, paintings, marble artefacts and carved capitals. In total, the palazzo has dozens (some say more than forty) rooms, each of which is meticulously decorated in an individual style – and with a certain flamboyance. The mirror-filled Ballroom contains finely decorated doors and overpoweringly elaborate stucco-work. Then come the Pink Room, the Red Room, the Yellow Room, the Green Room and the … run out of colours? … Middle Room (Salotto di Mezzo), each more sumptuously decorated than the next, and all with richly frescoed ceilings. Then there is the Council Chamber, with its gigantic fireplace, and the room that is the "apotheosis" of the entire palazzo: the Monumental Gallery, which is definitely more of a gallery than a salon, given that it's five times as long as it is wide. On entering you're overwhelmed by the unrestrained luxury of the place: there are huge mirrors with a myriad of ostentatious lamps, niches containing large statues, decorations in gold and white, the inevitable columns, and a large frescoed cupola – combining to make this one of the most luxurious interiors in Florence, indeed in Italy. This was exactly the intention of Camillo Borghese, husband of Pauline Bonaparte. When he undertook the complete refurbishment of this palazzo in 1822, he didn't hesitate to spend a fortune on the project, employing the city's very best craftsmen and creating a centrepiece for Florentine high society. Later Prince Poniatowski of Poland opened the Casino Borghese here. After extensive restoration in the 1990s, the building is now only open for receptions and other social events.

ORATORY OF THE COMPAGNIA DI SAN NICCOLÒ AL CEPPO

Children's Oratory

Via de' Pandolfini, 2
Open Monday–Friday, from 5pm to 7pm
Donations welcome

At the beginning of Via de' Pandolfini is a small door set in a roughcast wall with no decoration or identifying sign; this is the entrance to the now almost forgotten Compagnia di San Niccolò al Ceppo,* one of the oldest confraternities in Florence. Originally set up in the fourteenth century, its premises were located at various places in the city before being transferred here in 1561.

Initially established to provide catechism for the young people of Florence during the day and prayer meetings for adults (in particular, artisan workers) during the late afternoon, the confraternity is still active, although now restricted to offering Mass in this oratory.

Open to all, the oratory has a small vestibule which leads through into a warm and welcoming room with simple wood furnishings and a ceiling with frescoes by Giandomenico Ferretti depicting *Scenes from the Life of St Nicholas*. The *Crucifixion* over the high altar is by Francesco Curradi and replaces what was the oratory's artistic masterpiece: a *Crucifixion with St Nicholas and St Francis* formerly attributed to Fra Angelico but now thought to be the work of Paolo Uccello. (It is now in San Marco museum.) There are also two paintings by the sixteenth-century painter Giovanni Antonio Sogliani: *The Visitation* and *St Nicholas with Two Children of the Compagnia*;

these were used during religious processions as the confraternity's banners.

If you'd like to become a member of the confraternity you can join by paying a small fee in the secretary's office. Quite apart from the "spiritual benefit" this affords, you'll then feel you really belong to this charming oratory. The space has recently been rediscovered as a venue for theatre productions, and even when it's still and quiet, the welcoming atmosphere gives some idea of what it must have been like when Florentine youngsters filled these rooms.

Ceppo (trunk) refers to the tree trunk that was hollowed out to receive the offerings of the faithful.

PALAZZO DEI VISACCI

Baccio Valori's urban pantheon

Borgo degli Albizi, 18
Interior closed to the public

The well-known sardonic wit of the Florentines has targeted Palazzo Valori-Altoviti (more commonly known as Palazzo dei Visacci). The numerous statues erected by its owner, Baccio Valori, reflect the tastes of a born intellectual. As well as celebrities, he had a predilection for obscure scholars, and in return people laughed at those "ugly mugs" (*visacci*) reproduced on the façade. Baccio entrusted the task of creating the desired pantheon of images to sculptor Giovanni Battista Caccini, who between 1660 and 1664 installed fifteen *stiacciato* (relief) monuments, five on each of the three storeys.

The result is an open-air gallery, with jurist Accursio, monk Pietro Torrigiano Rustichelli, Neoplatonist Marsile Ficino, writer and humanist Donato Acciaiuoli, philologist Piero Vettori (first floor); navigator Amerigo Vespucci, architect Leon Battista Alberti, historian Francesco Guicciardini, humanist Marcello Adriani, philologist Vincenzo Borghini (second floor); and Giovanni della Casa (from Mugello), author of

Il Galateo, writers Boccaccio, Dante and Petrarch, and poet-agronomist Luigi Alamanni (third floor). Baccio himself was given a commemorative plaque, although in an inner hall of the palazzo, while five other statues of equally celebrated personalities, including Lorenzo the Magnificent, stand in the vestibule.

The first floor is occupied by the headquarters of the Florence Masonic Lodge affiliated to the Grand Orient of Italy.

A plaque below a window records how the miracle of St Zenobia took place in AD 400, when the son of a Gallic pilgrim was resurrected in the Holy Land.

DIVINE COMEDY PLAQUES

A real treasure hunt?

In the streets of central Florence you'll find a total of thirty-four plaques with quotations from the *La Divina Commedia*: nine from *Inferno*, five from *Purgatorio* and no less than twenty from *Paradiso*. The latter are primarily related to the Florentine families that Dante mentions in the sixteenth *canto* of that work. Given their number and unity of form, these plaques form a sort of unfolding poetic mural that is unique in the world. However, although they are now considered to be an integral part of the "Stones of Florence", they actually date from a project initiated in 1900, when the City Council appointed a committee of three Dante experts (including Isidoro del Lungo) to identify: (1) lines within

the poem that are in direct relation to the city, either place names and geographical locations or with respect to the characters depicted; (2) the most suitable – and most accurate – places to site such plaques. Seven years were enough for the entire project to be completed, thus setting the seal on the relationship between the poet and the city which raised and then exiled him.

Inferno VIII, 61–63 (Filippo Argenti): Via del Corso, location of the home of the Adimai, parents of Filippo Argenti;

Inferno X, 58–63 (Guido Cavalcanti): Via Calzaiuoli, location of the home of the Cavalcanti;

Inferno X, 91–93 (Farinata): Palazzo Vecchio, first courtyard;

Inferno XII, 146 (Arno): small loggia of Ponte Vecchio;

Inferno XV, 82–87 (Brunetto Latini): Via Cerretani, Church of Santa Maria Maggiore, location of the tomb of Brunetto Latini;

Inferno XVII, 58–60 (Gianfigliazzi): Via Tornabuoni, location of the home of the Gianfigliazzi;

Inferno XIX, 17 (Baptistery): Baptistery, looking towards Via Martelli;

Inferno XXIII, 94–95 (birth of the poet on the banks of the Arno): Via Dante Alighieri, Dante's house;

Inferno XXXII, 79–81, 106–108 (Bocca degli Abati): Via dei Tavolini, where the house of the Abati once stood;

Purgatorio XII, 100–105 (church of San Miniato al Monte and Ponte alle Grazie, formerly Ponte Rubaconte): at the beginning of Via San Salvatore al Monte;

Purgatorio XIV, 16–18 (Arno): Piazza Piave, tower of the Zecca Vecchia;

Purgatorio XXIV, 79–84 (Forese Donati): Via del Corso, near the ruins of Donati Tower;

Purgatorio XXIV, 82–87 (Corso Donati): Piazza San Salvi, where the troops of Henry VII camped near the monastery during the siege of Florence;

Purgatorio XXX, 31–33 (Beatrice Portinari): Via del Corso, location of the home of the Portinari;

Purgatorio XV, 97–99 (Florence): Via Dante Alighieri, near the Badia;

Paradiso XV, 112–114 (Belliccion Berti Ravignani): Via del Corso, location of the home of the Ravignani;

Paradiso XVI, 40–42 (Dante's ancestors): Via degli Speziali, location of the home of the Alighieri;

Paradiso XVI, 85–87 (Florentine dignitaries): Via delle Oche, market where the main families of Florence gathered each year;

Paradiso XVI, 94–96 (Cerchi family): Via del Corso, location of the home of the Cerchi;

Paradiso XVI, 101–102 (Galigai family): Via dei Tavolini, location of the home of Galigai;

Paradiso XV, 109–110 (Uberti family): Palazzo Vecchio, first courtyard;

Paradiso XVI, 110–111 (Lamberti family): Via Lamberti;

Paradiso XVI, 112–114 (Visdomini family): Via delle Oche, alongside the ruins of Visdomini Tower;

Paradiso XVI, 115–117 (Adimari family): Via delle Oche, location of the home of Adimari;

Paradiso XVI, 125–126 (Peruzzi family, with symbol of six pears): Borgo dei Greci, location of a gateway on city ramparts;

Paradiso XVI, 127–128, 130–132 (Della Bella family): Via dei Cerchi, location of the home of the Della Bella;

Paradiso XVI, 127–130 (Ugo di Brandeburgo): Via del Proconsolo, location of the Badia, a church where a commemoration service for Ugo di Brandeburgo, called Ugo di Toscana, is still held every 21 December;

Paradiso XVI, 133–135 (Gualterotti family): Borgo Sant'Apostoli, location of the home of Gualterotti;

Paradiso XVI, 136–139 (Amidei family): Via Por Santa Maria, alongside the ruins of Amidei Tower;

Paradiso XVI, 140–144 (Buondelmonti): Borgo Sant'Apostoli, location of the home of Buondelmonti;

Paradiso XVI, 145–147 (remains of the statue of Mars): Ponte Vecchio at the corner with Piazza del Pesce, where the remains of the statue once stood;

Paradiso XVI, 149–154 (old Florence): Palazzo Vecchio;

Paradiso XXV, 1–9 (baptism): Baptistery, looking towards the Duomo;

Paradiso XXXIII, 1–9 (St Bernard's prayer to the Virgin): Piazza del Duomo, but this last plaque has disappeared.

Oltrarno

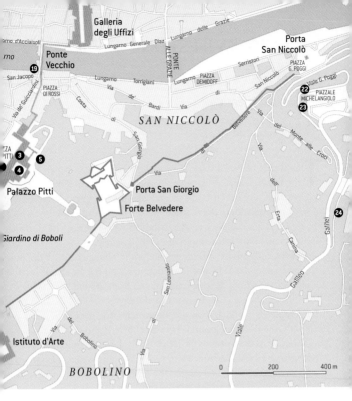

AN ENIGMA IN STONE AT PITTI PALACE

Concealed message

Pitti Palace
Piazza Pitti

The façade of Pitti Palazzo is powerfully seductive – in part because the frontage appears to extend beyond the field of vision of the naked eye. The very colour of the stones, whose ochre gives an impression of warmth, also adds to the charm of the building. And within the whole are set large, but slightly irregular, windows whose design and distribution reflects the aesthetic canons of the Renaissance.

However, the most striking feature is the arrangement of the protruding rectangular blocks of stone that make up the façade: of varying degrees of regularity, these decrease in size from ground level upwards. This change gives the impression that the stones towards the base were less completely worked, with the blocks acquiring greater finish as the building rose from the ground. However, there is also an enigma in the organisation of the stones of the façade: in the lower section there are two incongruous blocks, one much longer than the others, one much shorter.

It seems that when Luca Pitti had these two stones inserted here he intended that the larger should be identified as himself, and the shorter seen as a derogatory reference to his business rivals, jealous both of his financial success and this huge new palazzo. So this is a "mural jibe". And whether or not this story is true, it's surely no accident that a stone measuring 12 metres in length was set alongside one measuring just half a metre.

It's amusing to try and spot them yourself. But here's a tip: look to the left of the central doorway, between the projecting stone blocks about 2 metres from ground level.

NEARBY ②

Piazza Pitti, 1702

Piazza Pitti 7
Via dei Serragli 99
Via dei Cerretani 10
Via Porta Rossa 12

1702? Seeing is believing. Above the door of the building standing just opposite Pitti Palazzo are two numbers: 7 and 1702.

Which is the right one?

The 1702 is perhaps the last remaining trace of the old system for numbering Florence's houses, in which N°1 was Ponte Vecchio itself.

This single system extended in a capillary fashion throughout the city, following an even more complex logic than that found in the street numbers of Venice, where at least the buildings are divided according to *sestieri* (the six districts that make up the city).

In Oltrarno, the first building was numbered 1289, with the numbers also continuing on the other side of the river, reaching beyond 8000 in the Santa Croce district.

The whole system was reformed in 1865, introducing the present numbering by street or piazza.

This was when the building once numbered 1702 became 7 Piazza Pitti.

As for the old system, it's nothing but a memory, although traces can still pose the odd puzzler for the sharp-eyed visitor.

Florentine street numbers

There are two systems of street numbers in Florence: private residences have dark blue numbers, while public buildings and business premises have red numbers. As each system follows its own numerical order, it is possible for example to see a blue No. 25 alongside a red No. 3. The addresses given in this guide respect this special numbering system – when the number is that of business premises, it is followed by the letter "r".

GRAND-DUCAL KITCHEN AT THE PITTI PALACE

Buontalenti's fireplace

Piazza dei Pitti, 1
Open Tuesday–Sunday from 8.15am to 6.50pm
Itinerary of the Palatine Gallery (accompanied by a member of staff), Tuesday
and Sunday: mornings at 10.30 and 11.30 and afternoons at 3.30 and 4.30

The itinerary of the Pitti Palace guided tour has recently been expanded to include the restored historic grand-ducal kitchen. These new facilities were built in 1588 at the initiative of Ferdinando 1 de' Medici, to replace those in the monumental courtyard. The work was completed in summer 1599 so that the kitchen would be operational in time for the marriage of Marie de Médicis, daughter of the late Francesco I, to Henry IV of France. This marriage, which took place in October 1600, was the occasion for sumptuous banquets celebrated in both Palazzo Vecchio and the Pitti Palace. The new kitchen was sited outside the palace, connected by a covered walkway on the first floor. The rooms that have survived are however only part of the original sixteenth-century buildings, known as the "court" or "secret" kitchen (*la cucina segreta*), which was used to prepare meals for the grand duke and his guests. Even today, this kitchen is distinguished by its magnificent fireplace with a lintel of oblique dressed stones, probably based on a drawing by Buontalenti, who as well as being an architect, sculptor and painter was a noted gourmet. Between 1631 and 1640, this set of rooms was incorporated into the extension of the royal palace on the Via Romana side. During the Habsburg-Lorraine period, new ovens and hoods were added and the walls were covered with ceramic tiles with floral motifs, probably from the Ginori factory, to make a "royal kitchen" of it. Most of the utensils on display in the space open to the public are from the equipment supplied by the House of Savoy when the capital of the Kingdom of Italy was transferred to Florence and the Pitti Palace became the new royal residence.

Sixteenth-century air conditioning

In order to cope with the intense summer heat, the Medici assigned some of their court architects the task of designing a system to cool down the rooms of the Pitti Palace. This was achieved by taking advantage of the shady Boboli Gardens behind the palace, from where fresh air was conveyed to a basement room. From there, it was distributed by a system of channels and basins of icy water to each of the rooms on the upper floors of the residence, effectively lowering the temperature by about 10 degrees.

MONUMENT TO A MULE

④

An animal that died of exhaustion

Pitti Palace courtyard
Open Tuesday–Sunday from 8.15am to 6.50pm
Closed every Monday, Christmas Day, New Year's Day and May 1

Stroll down to the bottom left of Pitti Palace courtyard and you'll discover a bas-relief dedicated to an animal: one of the mules or donkeys that transported the building materials to the site when the palace was being constructed. The poor beast was forced to work so hard that it dropped dead with fatigue. At least it was honoured by a monument with this eloquent epitaph: *Lettighe, pietre e marmi, legnami, colonne / portò, tirò e trasportò anche questa lapide* (Litters, stone and marble, wood, columns / it carried, it dragged and it also transported this tombstone). This monument is also of interest because of the contemporary site details it depicts: workmen, ropes, winches, pulleys, capitals beings raised, workbenches. But despite this abundance of detail, no thought has been given to whether the mule was male or female: there's no indication of its sex in this sculpture.

The ambassador's horse

Far from the Pitti Palace is a commemorative plaque dedicated to another animal: the famous "ambassador's horse" belonging to Venetian Carlo Cappello, who, on the death of his four-legged friend, had a plaque erected in its memory on the Lungarno Anna Maria dei Medici near Piazza dei Giudici. He wrote the eulogy himself. The horse also had the right to a solemn funeral, an honour not known to have been bestowed on the Pitti Palace mule.

SYMBOLISM OF THE STATUE OF "BACCHUS RIDING A TORTOISE"

A spiritual symbol inspired by the hermetic arts?

Boboli Gardens

In the Boboli Gardens – near the entrance to the left of Palazzo Pitti – is a curious fountain showing an overweight male figure riding a tortoise. Setting aside the tone of playful burlesque which was such an integral part of Florentine Mannerist architecture, you might read this statue as combining traditional symbolism and a concealed meaning.

For the Greeks and Romans, Bacchus was the god of wine (here represented by the water of the fountain) and was popularly associated with the orgies that might result from drunkenness. But at a symbolic level, these libations might be associated with inebriating Wisdom, which plunges those who partake of it into an ecstatic state. This means that Wisdom might be represented either by the vine or by the wine it produces. Indeed, since the earliest centuries of Christianity, wine had been seen as a symbol of *gnosis*, of divine Wisdom. Bacchus, in fact, was frequently associated with the Phoenician god Baal, "the Supreme Lord", whilst his Greek name, Dionysus, means "God with us".

Thus Bacchus represents the Supreme Godhead (the equivalent of Ganesh in Hinduism), what the Christian Gnostics of the third to fifth century AD called *Christus-Baal*. When Greek civilisation was at its height, the bacchantes were, in fact, chaste virgin priestesses dedicated to the veneration of the god of Wisdom. It was only later, when traditional symbols became distorted and traditional social values deformed, that Bacchus became the god of bacchanals, of excess, in a society that had itself become decadent.

Shown riding a tortoise, Bacchus becomes a symbol of the Supreme Godhead leading his creation: the Universe. In fact, for the Greeks and Romans, the tortoise was the symbol of a universe made manifest by the power of the Spirit (what the Hindus call *Purusha*) and thus symbolises the Throne of God.

Similarly, the tortoise was a symbol of the Great Work of hermetism, which was based on the three main chemical elements of Sulphur, Mercury and Salt. Sulphur was associated with the head of the tortoise (symbolising Heaven or the Upper Level); the shell suggested the Earth (or Middle Level) and was associated with Mercury. Finally there was the tortoise's belly, an emblem of Hell and the Lower Level associated with Salt.

Alchemy and the Hermetic Arts in the Boboli Gardens

Both Cosimo and Francesco de' Medici are known to have been interested in alchemy and the hermetic arts, with the Boboli Gardens and the Pitti Palace being just two of the places within the city where you can find traces of this interest. Apart from the statue of Bacchus on a tortoise (see opposite), another such trace is to be found on the raised walkway between Palazzo Vecchio and Palazzo Pitti, a walkway that Cosimo I commissioned Vasari to design. It is a depiction of a lion wearing a crown adorned at the front with a *fleur-de-lis*.

A symbol of power and light, the lion was associated with the sun and, as the King of the Animals, was seen as embodying strength, wisdom and justice. A guarantee of temporal power and a representation of spiritual power, the lion adorned not only the throne of Solomon but also that of kings in France, Italy and numerous other countries; in the Middle Ages, it also figured upon the thrones of bishops. In medieval iconography, the head and upper body of the lion were taken to embody the divine nature of Christ, whilst the lower part of the body represented his human nature. These two natures were represented by a bridge that was seen as running from the human to the divine and vice versa. In alchemy, the "crowned Lion" represents gold, the solar metal. Furthermore, the sign of Leo is set right at the heart of the zodiac. Within the Boboli Gardens there are also columns bearing depictions of reptiles, which some say are lizards, and others dragons. Two of them are intertwined and seem to be fighting, forming the traditional circle "of eternity" which the hermetists called ourob-

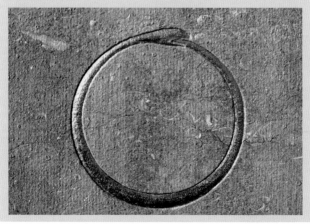

oros (the serpent which bites its tail: ob means "serpent" in Hebrew whilst ouro means "king" in Coptic).

This symbolises the resurrection of he who is reborn to a new spiritual life after sloughing off his mortal human condition. In the gardens immediately in front of Palazzo Pitti, an obelisk stands by the side of a water basin. The obelisk, in fact, has the stylised form of Celtic menhirs and ancient Egyptian pyramids. It was said to function as a catalyst of celestial energy and as a condenser of terrestrial energy – what in the East is known as *Fohat and Kundalini* and in the West as "sidereal tellurism" and "planetary tellurism".

A central junction where these two types of energy are concentrated, the obelisk thus generates vitality in the surrounding area and in those who walk around it. This revitalisation is here represented by the circular water basin. This symbolises the Ocean of Life, the living waters of creation over which the Divine Spirit moved, indicated by the primordial energies captured by the obelisk. In alchemy, that obelisk represents the phases in the Great Work which link together Earth and Heaven, the solid and the subtle, Matter and Spirit. Finally, it indicates the gradual passage from an imperfect state to the raised state of Perfect Being, a veritable "Philosopher of Fire". This state of Perfection is represented inside the palace by the *Fontana della Coppa*, which is surmounted by an infant at whose feet is a bird that looks like the phoenix. This is an anthropomorphic rendition of the Divine Heir who, in the Great Work, corresponds to the Philosopher's Stone, the ultimate aim of alchemy and symbolised by the phoenix. Thus, for those who know how to look, Palazzo Pitti is rich in sacred significance, the silent language of symbols revealing itself to be rich and expressive once its mysteries are unveiled.

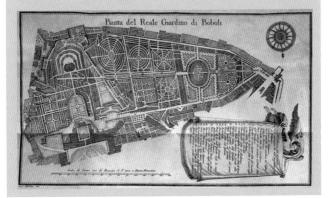

Pianta del Reale Giardino di Boboli

CASA GUIDI

Love nest of two poets

Piazza San Felice, 8
Tel: 055 354457
Open April 1–November 30 on Monday, Wednesday and Friday from 3pm to 6pm
Admission free but donations welcome
To book the building for a night, consult the site
http://bookings/landmarktrust.org.uk

C asa Guidi, largely unknown to tourists and locals, is a place of charming alike simplicity. While offering nothing extraordinary, it does give you some idea of the elegant retirement and intellectual peace enjoyed here by its two most illustrious residents. In fact, this apartment is reminiscent of the heyday of the English community in Florence. In a way it should be called Casa Browning, because in 1847 it was rented by one of the most extraordinary poetic couples in the history of literature: Robert Browning and his wife, Elizabeth Barrett Browning (she actually died here in 1861). Apart from a few fine mirrors, the contents of the house are of no particular value: the Brownings bought almost all their furniture from local second-hand dealers. However, the interiors that are still open to the public, more than 150 years later, reveal the sobriety and taste with which they decorated their living space. Indeed, the restoration carried out here by The Landmark Trust and Eton College was predicated on the desire to maintain the full character of the original, with the same woodwork, the same fireplace and the same colours in the painted and roughcast surfaces. Thus a perfectly intact period residence is waiting to be discovered here, complete with bedroom (containing the Brownings' piano), small study, convivial kitchen and charming library. Two busts and two painted portraits give some idea of the affable appearance of Robert Browning and the more austere physiognomy of his wife Elizabeth, whose face is shown framed by thick brown hair. There are also various objects that conjure up some sense of their private life together. The plaque on the outside wall has an inscription by Nicolò Tommaseo, recalling the role this remarkable couple played in consolidating the bond between Britain and Italy at a time when the first wave of British artists was arriving to search for inspiration on the banks of the Arno.

Night at Casa Guidi

One of the two bedrooms in the apartment can be rented (maximum six people). An unforgettable way to pass a night in Florence.

ASTRONOMICAL TOWER OF LA SPECOLA

⑦

Long-forgotten observatory

Via Romana, 17
www.msn.unifi.it
Visits by appointment only, with paid guide; cost of guide in addition to
admission fee
To book, call 055 2346760 Monday–Friday from 10am to 2pm, or e-mail
edumsn@unifi.it

Even though *specola* is an old Italian word for "observatory", few know that the present Museo della Specola was for a long time Florence's Astronomical Observatory. The observatory tower was once a key point of reference for the scientific community within the city. Curiously enough, however, the Specola Observatory was built at the foot of a hill rather than on the summit, which would have been a much better place from which to observe the heavens, but the aim was to encourage links between scientific activities in the city centre.

The observatory entered into service in 1807, furnished with the most up-to-date equipment and run by renowned scholars. However, it had been planned at the end of the eighteenth century, a period in which a large number of elementary scientific criteria were still unknown. Nevertheless, the Specola Observatory achieved a number of results that established its reputation within the European scientific community. For example, between 1855 and 1857, it identified three comets and carried out various metrological studies that confirmed the discoveries made by the Accademia del Cimento from the mid-seventeenth century onwards. Ultimately, its poor location meant that the observatory proper had to relocate to Arcetri. As a result, the various rooms of this building – including the meridian room and the octagonal room allowing for 360° observation of the heavens – fell into disuse, and the place was virtually forgotten. After long and painstaking restoration, the old observatory was reopened in 2009, allowing the public to rediscover this exceptional room. However, if you want to observe the stars it is still better to go up to Arcetri.

The only trace of the sixteen Florentine gonfalons

On the wall of Via Sant'Agostino, you can still see a stone plaque engraved with a dragon and a whip. This is the only evidence in the whole city of the old Florentine gonfalons (standards or banners). The medieval city's four main districts, which have survived thanks to the *calcio storico*, were subdivided into so many gonfalons – like the *contrade* that race in the Palio di Siena. Santo Spirito had a whip as its emblem and San Frediano a dragon. The stone in what is now Via Sant'Agostino indicated the boundary between the whip and the dragon districts.

SALONE DEGLI SCHELETRI

Museum of horrors

Museo della Specola
Via Romana, 17
www.msn.unifi.it
Open 9.30am to 4.30pm; closed Monday, 1 January, Easter Sunday,
1 May, 15 August and 25 December
Admission to the museum: €6 (full price) and €3 (concessions) • Admission
to the Skeleton Room, requiring telephone booking (055 2346760), Monday–
Saturday from 9am to 5pm, according to availability
Cost of the (obligatory) guided tour: €30 for groups up to a maximum of thirty

The Museo della Specola is a little gem. First there are the anatomical statues in wax by Susini and Ferrini – one of the rare collections in the world, although there are two other little-known examples in Paris and Venice (see our guides *Secret Paris* and *Secret Venice*). But this museum also has a depiction of a decomposing head, which the Syracuse-born artist Zumbo based on a real skull; some rather disturbing *teatri della peste* (plague theatres); and a collection of stuffed animals. Furthermore, in what used to be the stables on the ground floor, you can now once more visit the astonishing Salone degli Scheletri (Skeleton Room 55), an even more staggering space that has been closed to the public for years. With a name that sounds like the title of a horror film, this room has a spectacular collection of animal skeletons contained within 120 glass display cases, arranged like so many huge pieces of furniture. The largest are those of a whale (a sperm whale to be precise) and an elephant, the former suspended from the ceiling to form a sort of aerial exhibit, and the latter set in the centre of the room. There are also various human skeletons – those of a woman, several men and a number of children. The 40 metre by 7 metre space itself gives the impression of extended perspective, which means that the skeletons have an even more dramatic impact. A period loggia provides further raised exhibition space, thus heightening the impression of being completely surrounded by skeletons. The room is sometimes used for night-time performances.

SALA DELLE CICOGNE

Storks in full flight

Astronomical Tower of La Specola
Museo della Specola
Via Romana, 17
www.msn.unifi.it
Visits by appointment only, with paid guide; cost of guide in addition to
admission fee
To book, call 055 2346760 Monday–Friday from 10am to 2pm,
or e-mail edumsn@unifi.it

The "telegraphic-system" meridian in the Specola is almost unique in the world. The only other known meridians of this type are to be found in Bologna and Budapest. Located in the Sala delle Cicogne (Stork Room), this meridian was – together with the astronomical and meteorological observatories – part of the scientific apparatus of the Museo Imperiale e Reale di Fisica e di Storia Naturale that was set up in 1775 by Grand Duke Piero Leopoldo I. Stretched between two clamps at 60 millimetres above ground level, a metal wire (once a thread of woven hair) traced a line parallel to the meridian. The technical precision here was ultimately nullified by the changes in ground level over the years. Looking at the wire, the meridian could be read on the band of marble and copper on the floor; at the centre of this band runs a thread of silver marked by the signs of the zodiac, which are not merely decorative but indicate the point that corresponds to the passage of the Sun through the various constellations. This meridian also allowed an observer to identify solstices and solar eclipses, which are indicated by refined depictions of a shining Sun. High up on the wall can be seen the small hole where the ray of sunlight that served as the gnomon entered. Finally, there is the rail-mounted equipment which made it possible to slide a telescope along the axis of the meridian for nocturnal observations; these involved another astronomical instrument called  a *quarantale*. Remarkable for its various scientific uses as well as its aesthetic qualities, the meridian is located in a room which itself demonstrates how the arts and sciences go together: the Sala delle Cicogne is decorated with a wealth of precious materials and admirable stucco-work depicting twenty storks in full flight.

For more informations about sundials, see page 75.

CORSI ANNALENA GARDEN

Hanging garden of Oltrarno

Via dei Serragli, 133
Visits by kind permission of the owners
Tel: 055 2280105 or e-mail scarsellistefania@yahoo.it

Modest in size, the Corsi Annalena garden is laid out in terraces overlooking Via dei Serragli, terracing undoubtedly being the best way of organising a garden when there is little surface area. The result affords a panoramic view of the countryside around Florence, extending from the urban fabric itself to the vast green area of Parco dei Torrigiani and the hills beyond. There is even an underground passageway linking this garden to the Boboli and to the Parco dei Torrigiani, making it possible to get from the Pitti Palace to the countryside beyond the city walls without being disturbed. However, this is only one of the secrets of this garden, which owes its name to Countess Anna Elena Malatesta. In the fifteenth century she had a monastery built here, which was subsequently destroyed by Cosimo I as a defensive measure during a war with the Sienese.

Later the site was acquired by the Corsi family, who at the beginning of the nineteenth century commissioned Giuseppe Manetti to design the layout of what would be the first "Romantic" garden in the city, complete with all the associated amenities. You can anticipate what lies inside the garden from the external corner between Via Romana and Via de' Mori, where stands a Tempio del Canto (Temple of Song). A good 3 metres above pavement level – thus revealing the raised level of the garden itself – this "kiosk" is complete with a niche for a statue of Mercury, the god of travellers, who stood there to welcome the visitors who entered Florence by the Siena road. The entire garden is, in fact, full of statues – from a complete series of *The Muses* in terracotta to a copy of Verrocchio's *Putto with Dolphin*. There is also a greenhouse, a fountain

and, alongside the terrace, decorative stucco-work and a semicircular bench in wrought iron. This admirable garden forms a wonderful aesthetic ensemble – and it is well worth applying to the owners for permission to visit.

GIARDINO TORRIGIANI

(11)

Oltrarno's private park

Via dei Serragli
Visits, lasting 1½ hours, are organised on request;
contact susanna@giardinotorrigiani.it or call 349 2868449
www.giardinotorrigiani.it

Torrigiani is more than just a private garden, it is a proper park: the wonderful open space extends over 6 hectares of land between the old city walls in Viale Petrarca and Via dei Serragli. Indeed, at one time it actually covered a total of 10 hectares, thanks to various land purchases made by the Torrigianis in the years 1802–17.

It was Luigi Cambray Digny – later followed by Gaetano Baccani – who designed this park, which has a rich variety of plants and numerous decorative features – from trimmed hedges to geometrical layouts and stage-set style avenues. Note Pio Fede's neoclassical monument dedicated to Piero Torrigiani, and the large neo-Gothic tower. The tower was the work of Baccani himself and is complete with an external spiral staircase and a small observation platform at the top. It has actually become one of the symbols of Oltrarno – even if the Florentines themselves only catch a glimpse of it on the other side of the park walls.

FRANCIABIGIO'S *LAST SUPPER*

The only Last Supper *still in a working refectory*

Monastero della Calza
Piazza della Calza, 6
Open daily 2pm to 3.30pm
Book at least a day in advance; by phone at 05 222 287 or write to calza@calza.it
Guided tours can be organised
Closed during the week of August 15
Admission free

The most unusual *Last Supper* in Florence is by the Italian Renaissance painter Franciabigio, who may be less famous than others who have tackled this classic theme but whose highly original work does have the distinction of being the only one still hanging in a working refectory (the dining room of the youth hostel run by the Monastero della Calza).

However, you don't have to be a guest here to view the work, which is remarkably dynamic in composition. Judas, undoubtedly touched by Christ's words, is so troubled that he appears about to upset the salt cellar and knock over the stool on which he is sitting; the other apostles are shown caught up in discussion, with one about to rise from the table; and the wind seems to have caught one of the window shutters. In contrast to all this, St John rests his head on Christ's right shoulder – a gesture of calm intimacy.

Florence's eight *Last Suppers*

Dating from 1514, Franciabigio's dynamic composition should be compared with the eight other frescoes of *The Last Supper* in Florence (more than any city in the world). These works are dotted across the city map like the stars of a constellation, featuring in the old city centre, in the Oltrarno district and even in suburban areas. You could visit them all, one after the other, to appreciate their variations on the theme – beginning for example with Andrea del Sarto's work at San Salvi, followed by Ghirlandaio's two *Last Suppers* at Ognissanti and the Monastery of San Marco, Andrea del Castagno's at Sant'Apollonia and Taddeo Gaddi's at Santa Croce. The lesser-known works are Andrea Orcagna's at Santo Spirito, Fuligno's at Sant'Onofrio and this Franciabigio at the Monastero della Calza. The variety is explained by the rivalry between the Florentine monasteries and convents, and its art patrons – whose tastes may even be reflected in the trees or dishes depicted in these frescoes.gli alberi o addirittura per i cibi raffigurati nel dipinto.

Architectural optical illusions

Among Florence's many windows painted in trompe l'oeil is a unique series (classified by the Directorate General of Fine Arts) at No. 18 Via del Campuccio. On the façade of a small mansion are three windows: the first is painted, as is its finely worked black grille. The second is identical to the first, but with a real grille over a real window. The third is an unusual compromise, with grille and window part-real and part-painted.

MUSEO DI SIMBOLOGIA MASSONICA⑬

Esoteric aprons

Via dell'Orto, 7
Open Tuesday–Friday from 3pm to 7pm, and Saturday–Sunday
from 10am to 1pm and 3pm to 7pm
Tel: 055 220166
www.musma.firenze.it

In 2012, in the city of Italy's first Masonic lodge and of Collodi's *Pinocchio* – a fable of initiation into life dissimulated as Masonic ritual –a keen collector opened the Museum of Masonic Symbols. It has a still-growing collection of Freemasonry arcana.

At the entrance, visitors may be asked whether they are "initiates" or simply "curious". The explanations then given will vary depending on the visitor's affiliation to Freemasonry and knowledge of the symbolism that follows from initiation. For those who can decipher the meaning of the exhibits, this museum is a goldmine. Although perhaps a tad repetitive for the secular public, the collection is still fascinating. You'll find all sorts of things: dozens of drawers that can be opened to look through vintage photos and certificates of the various Masonic grades and bodies or "obediences", stylised paintings and a vast quantity of medals, ritual objects and symbols, as well as stamps featuring Masonic characters or themes, porcelain, glass, pamphlets and books. But what makes this museum a Europe-wide attraction for Freemasonry enthusiasts is the range of ceremonial aprons, one of the largest collections of such regalia in the world, with several thousand pieces. Exhibited with an assortment of banners and other items of clothing, most of these aprons date from the nineteenth century and come mainly from the United States, though some are from Europe and other parts of the world. Drawings and mottoes have been embroidered in the most diverse languages. They invite you to discover the origins of the lodges, each tracing the history of a secret and often extraordinary community, such as the Italian lodges of Argentina or the Minnesota Indians. Many are true masterpieces, judging by the details of the images and the associations of colours, on red, purple, black, blue or polychrome backgrounds. If you're only expecting to see compasses and set squares, you'll soon change your mind

in view of the iconographic richness of the collection. Like a real initiatory journey, the tour ends in a room with a small reconstruction of a Masonic temple where the innumerable symbols of the museum objects seem to fall into place in a more hushed and intimate atmosphere.

For more informations about Pinocchio and the masonry, see next page.

Pinocchio: the first Masonic puppet

Though not officially recognised, Carlo Collodi's membership in the Freemasons is widely believed to be confirmed by a range of evidence: he started a satirical newspaper entitled *Il Lampione* (The Lamp Post) in 1848, with the express aim of "illuminating all those held in thrall by the shadows"; his participation in the campaigns of Giuseppe Garibaldi, a famous *carbonaro* advocating liberal ideas and undoubtedly a Mason; his close relationship with Mazzini, who was a well-known Mason and of whom Collodi declared himself to be a "passionate disciple". Furthermore, the guiding principles of the Freemasons – *Liberty, Equality and Fraternity* – are embodied in T*he Adventures of Pinocchio*: Liberty, because Pinocchio is a free being, who loves liberty; Equality, because Pinocchio's sole aspiration is to be equal to everyone else, accepting that all are born equal to each other; Fraternity, because this is the feeling that seems to motivate the characters at various points in the story. *Pinocchio* was also immortalised in a film by the American Walt Disney, himself a high-ranking Mason, and embodies the three founding principles of universal Freemasonry: freedom of thought and will; psychological and social equality; fraternity between individuals, who can thus achieve universal understanding. More than a simple children's story, Pinocchio is an initiatory tale, as is Goethe's *Faust* and Mozart's *The Magic Flute*. It can be read at various levels as a Masonic parable, with the multiple meanings reflecting themes and formulas associated with the stages of initiation. Indeed, it is due to these veiled allusions to an initiatory path that Pinocchio owes its extraordinary success (its sales in twentieth-century Italy were second only to those of *La Divina Commedia*), for the various stages in the plot offer subliminal echoes of cognitive archetypes. A formidable didactic instrument, *Pinocchio* takes its place alongside the official educational literature of its day. A moral tale deeply imbued with the message of political emancipation, it is one of Tuscan culture's greatest contributions to Freemasonry. Pinocchio is subject to a long course of development. Initially nothing more than a "rough" piece of wood (just like the "rough" stone that all the uninitiated have to cut and shape), he must become "polished" (a term which in the Masonic vocabulary means "enlightened"). The very name of Pinocchio derives from *pinolo*, the Italian word for "pine nut", thus there is a connection with pine trees, traditionally associated with Christmas – and Christmas itself is a symbol of the spiritual rebirth that the neophyte will experience when he receives the light of initiation. Furthermore, it is no coincidence that the central character of the tale, Geppetto, is a carpenter, as was Joseph, the father who raised Jesus Christ. As a carpenter, Geppetto is also a demiurge ("creator", "artisan") in the Platonic and Gnostic sense of the term. A little later in the tale, the Blue Fairy descends from heaven to teach Pinocchio free will, and when he asks if he has finally become a real boy she significantly answers: "No, Pinocchio. The vow of your father Geppetto will not fully come true until you deserve it. Set yourself to the test, with courage, sincerity and passion, and one day you will become a real little boy." This is precisely what is said during Masonic initiation, with regard to apprenticeship and the bearing of responsibility. The voice of the Cricket is definitely that of conscience, urging the puppet to go "to school" – another Masonic symbol for conscience and awareness. The initiation of Pinocchio also comprises a series of trials that involve all four elements: air (the presence of numerous birds in the story, and the puppet's flight on the wings of a dove); earth (the coins buried in the ditch); fire (which burns his feet) and water (with various episodes, right up to the final chapter, involving swimming and drowning). Pinocchio is also prey to "sleep", another Masonic metaphor for the non-activity of the uninitiated; and it is precisely when he is asleep that the Blue Fairy gives him a kiss (a kiss also being part of the Masonic rite of the Templars). When hanged, Pinocchio dies, but he is resuscitated through a purge/purification – that is, by elevating himself to a higher level of initiation. Among the other references to Freemasonry there is the island of industrious bees, which recalls Hiram's Temple of Solomon, with its four hundred pomegranates. That is also the exact number of the small bread buns which the Blue Fairy prepares together with cups of coffee and milk (the colour contrast of black and white is another feature of the Temple and a symbol of the contrast between good and evil). The Cat, the Fox and the Firefly all embody the temptations of an easy and profane life, with limping and lameness being other allusions to Masonic symbols. The puppeteer Stromboli and the Land of Toys again represent the vanities of this world, and Pinocchio's transformation into a donkey reveals he has fallen to the level of beasts. To save himself, he must return to the path of enlightenment. The puppet must find his father/demiurge, but he can only do so after passing through a biblical trial: being swallowed by a whale like Jonah, the central figure in a myth that is fundamental in all the great monotheistic religions and all schools of esotericism. Being reunited with Geppetto, who bears him on his shoulders as he swims through the primary element of water, Pinocchio finally becomes a "real little boy", one of the truly "enlightened".

ACCADEMIA BARTOLOMEO CRISTOFORI

Friends of the precursor of the piano

Via Camaldoli, 7r
Tel: 055 221646
www.accademiacristofori.it • info@accademiacristofori.it
The museum can be visited during concerts
Other visits, on payment and with a guided tour by a qualified musician,
can be booked by contacting 349 2653334, with at least two weeks' notice

At the heart of the San Frediano district, the green doorway at N° 7 (red) Via Camaldoli gives access to an old factory that has been refurbished by the architect Temistocle Antoniadis. The place now houses a veritable gem of Florentine cultural life, which is still largely unknown outside the district itself. This exemplary private institution is named after Bartolomeo Cristofori, the inventor of the pianoforte, and it would be difficult to find a place that offered a fuller range of services and events within a warmer or more welcoming atmosphere. The first part of the institute comprises a museum of the pianoforte, with various organs and numerous rare examples of this precursor of the modern-day instrument. Now long forgotten, the pianoforte had its own very particular sound and was made entirely from wood, without any metal reinforcements. Within the instrument, the hammers that strike the cords are padded with leather rather than felt (as in a modern piano), although it was possible, by means of a special pedal, to insert a piece of felt between the hammer and cord to obtain a more diaphanous sound, perfectly suited to the repertoire that runs from Mozart through Beethoven to Schubert. Another pedal, known as the Janissary or Turkish pedal, created a very resonant effect, while a third produced the sort of sonorities associated with the bassoon. Along with this remarkable collection of instru-

ments, the academy has a specialist library and a workshop renowned for its restoration of musical instruments. Most importantly there is also a hundred-seat auditorium used for the two main activities of this charming institution: a season of chamber music concerts (on average, two per month) and master classes given by highly skilled musicians. The "ABC", as the members of the academy like to refer to it, is open to the public during concerts and restoration projects, or on request for a private visit.

HISTORIC JEWISH CEMETERY ⑮

Old Jewish tombs in San Frediano

Viale Ariosto, 16
Open the first Sunday of each month, from 10am to 12pm
At extra cost, guided tours for groups can be organised outside usual opening
hours • Tel: 055 2346654

Like Venice, Florence has a historic Jewish cemetery, even if this one dates from rather later: 1777. At the foot of the city walls and just a short walk from the San Frediano Gateway, this sacred place is curiously surrounded by buildings of several storeys – hardly a setting that creates a meditative atmosphere – and is located near a nursery school. In fact built on land that once belonged to the cemetery, this school was the fruit of building speculation that verged on profanation. One result, for example, was that certain eighteenth-century gravestones were moved haphazardly to near the entrance to the cemetery, with most being set upside down by workmen who clearly couldn't read Hebrew. In line with Jewish tradition, there are neither images nor photographs of the deceased on the tombs. However, the tombs themselves are remarkably varied and it is this variety that makes the cemetery so eclectic and interesting. Along with simple gravestones and stelae, there are also tombs in the form of a sarcophagus or a small temple, or even an Egyptian pyramid (the Levi family tomb). Two other monumental tombs will certainly not pass unnoticed. One is a burial chapel designed by Treves, the architect of Florence's main synagogue, in the form of a sumptuously decorated colonnaded kiosk, while the other is a burial chapel in Egyptian style, which seems about to succumb to the weight of shrubbery covering it. The cemetery is resisting real-estate speculation as best it can. It was closed in 1870, after having been in existence for almost a century, and only recently has the decision been taken to reopen it to the public one day a month.

However, it still has a very neglected appearance. Nevertheless, the cypress-lined paths, the age of its strange tombs and the nonchalance that seems to be an integral part of Jewish culture, all retain the very particular charm of the place, in spite of its setting among the workaday buildings of this part of San Frediano.

TEMPO REALE

Crystalline notes of electronic music

Villa Strozzi
Via Pisani, 77
www.temporeale.it
Visits on request; info@temporerale.it; Tel: 055 717270; or during public events

Villa Strozzi stands on a hill overlooking Florence and its top floor is occupied by offices, artistic workshops and two "study spaces" that host events bearing witness to the long-standing relationship between the composer Luciano Berio and the city of Florence.

The Tempo Reale (Real Time) workshop that the famous composer founded remains a rare pearl in Italy. Reflecting a Florence very different to the usual "open-air museum", it demonstrates that the city can and must develop a future alongside its legendary past, participating fully in all the innovation made possible by modern technologies.

The researchers at this centre dedicated to electronic music have developed software for the "spatialisation" of sound, plus an instrument called a MEEG (Max Electronic Event Generator), which is used to programme works of electronic music, frequently for the centre's own productions. The entire scheme follows in the footsteps that Berio himself had taken within this new domain. In fact, his own compositions often figure in the events at Tempo Reale, which organises concerts; makes exceptional quality electronic instruments available to musicians and composers; and holds seminars and study workshops that are intended to "train" not only composers and orchestra musicians but also the general public.

A visit to the centre takes you through archives that are truly unique in Italy, offering the chance to see computers and other electronic instruments whose limitless musical potential is not immediately obvious.

In short, this is a trip into the future, amid the most remarkable sounds – and silences. Those who are already familiar with contemporary music will discover more about the ever-shifting boundaries of what can be achieved through the creative use of electronics. And, for those who are being introduced to such music for the first time, Tempo Reale offers a glimpse into a future of things never seen, sounds never heard – a world as mysterious as the process of creation itself.

ANTICO SETIFICIO FIORENTINO ⑰

Perfect silk

Via Bartolini, 4
Tel: 055 213861
www.anticosetificiofiorentino.it
Open Monday–Friday from 9am to 1pm and 2pm to 5pm

Access to the Antico Setifico Fiorentino is like something from a fairytale – through a gate and a silent garden. Inside is a craft workshop that stands comparison with any museum. Every corner of the place is rich in history, bearing witness to the skill – and power – of the glorious Arte della Seta (Silk Guild), one of those trade corporations that contributed to the wealth of Florence and to its reputation throughout Europe.

These premises in San Frediano became home to the guild in 1786, established thanks to the combined efforts of various Florentine families who obtained a licence to pursue the craft from the ruling powers of the day (first the grand duke, then the king).

Florence has been producing fine-quality silk since the fifteenth century, and despite competition from low-cost products on the international market, this ancient silkworks continues to manufacture fabrics using eighteenth-century looms and machines, old weave patterns and stencils, and hand-dyeing techniques. The range of patterns presently on offer has been updated on the basis of the fabrics to be seen in Renaissance and Mannerist paintings.

On display is a mule jenny, on which the thread was drawn from the skein and then wound around bobbins; a small cultural gem in itself, this seems to bridge the gap between craft tradition and industrialisation. And then, of course, there are the eighteenth-century looms.

Maintaining the tradition of Florentine silkmaking, this old silkworks has continued to innovate and add to its range of products, which now runs from original-style fabrics to high-quality modern-style upholstery. It also accepts individual commissions.

There's an amazing amount on offer at this workshop, where time seems to stand still.

FRESCOBALDI GARDEN

In the heart of Santo Spirito

Via Santo Spirito, 11
Tel: 055 211330
Visits on request to the caretaker on any day except Sunday, from 7.30am to
7.30pm, but preferably in the afternoon

The palazzo of the Frescobaldi was once referred to simply as Casa del Cortile (House with the Courtyard) because of the vast garden that is tucked away within it. Although hardly noticeable from the outside, the enclosed garden does have a stunning backdrop: a remarkable view of the wonderful church of Santo Spirito. In the first half of the seventeenth century, Matteo Frescobaldi decided to redevelop a number of properties in Via Santo Spirit that belonged to his family in order to build the present palazzo. Part of that work involved the layout of the garden that can be seen today. The approach is through a large porch that acts as a sort of airlock between the dense urban fabric of the old city centre and this haven of greenery so richly suited to meditation. Passing through this "decompression chamber", you enter one of those small private gardens that are the pride of central Florence, where artifice and nature seem to work together to create an oasis of silence and beauty. Until a few years ago the place was also graced with two bronze sculptures that admirably exemplified the work of the great Arnaldo Pomodoro. However, even if they have gone, there is still plenty to discover in this impeccably maintained *hortus clausus*: the lawn surrounded with azaleas; the statue of the god of Arcadia himself, Pan; and a large fountain modelled from monumental sponges (an architectural reminder of the period in which Casa del Cortile was built).

NEARBY
Florence's gondola ⑲
Arches of Ponte Vecchio

On the Oltrarno side of the bridge, a Venetian gondola can be seen moored most of the time near one of the piers, out of the way but clearly visible at water level (less so from the embankment). In winter, the vessel is generally covered with a tarpaulin, although it is left uncovered in summer. This fine boat belongs to a Florentine boat-owner, who – with the permission of the nearby Florence Rowing Club – uses it along the stretch of water that runs from Ponte Vecchio to Ponte alla Carraia.

ART ATHLETIC CENTER - SPORTS' MUSEUM

The history of sport recounted within a Florentine palazzo

Via Maggio, 39 • Free admission; visits by appointment
Tel: 055 217294

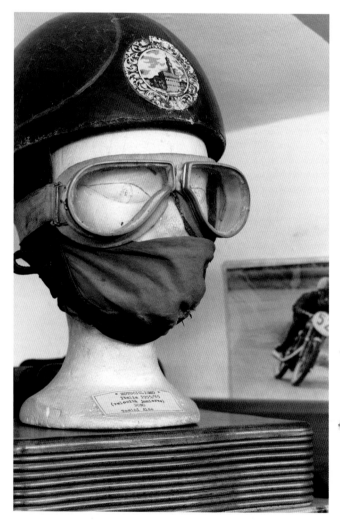

A museum of sports equipment is quite a rarity in Italy. But this one is made all the more special by the fact that it does not stand alongside some sports hall but is contained within a palazzo in the patrician Via Maggio – with an interior of Florentine terracotta floors and coffered ceilings. The owner of the place is himself an "original": Florentine by birth, he has managed to combine his activity as a weightlifter (an Italian record-holder in 1969) and his taste for collecting sports artefacts. Since the 1960s, he has put together a collection that offers a very representative picture of sporting customs and practices.

The 200 square metres of exhibition space are divided into two floors, and offer everything you might hope to find: from the inevitable fencing masks to curious "insect traps for fishing", from balls to riding equipment. There is even a perfect half-scale version of an early-twentieth-century FIAT sports car in black and red, as well as golf clubs and bicycles made by the French company Michaux in 1865.

Each piece of equipment illustrates the history of a sport and the passionate interest of its practitioners. Look, for example, at the range of wooden cylinders which were worn over the hand and used to knock a ball back and forth in the game of *pallone col bracciale*; it was for this sport that the City Council built the Fascine Sphaeristerium in 1895, a structure which is now a listed building.

Though not part of the obvious tourist circuit, this unusual museum has continued to grow since 1964. In itself, it exemplifies the sort of persistence and resolution that are typically Florentine – qualities that have enabled the owner of the house to put together a collection combining sport with art and history.

NEARBY

Structure of medieval shops ㉑

Borgo San Jacopo 66r

In this street is a rare example of how shops opened directly onto the street in the Middle Ages. Goods for sale were laid out on a stone counter where the price could be haggled over. The door, always to the left of the counter, led through to the shopkeeper's home – *uscio* e *bottega* ("door and shop"), as the saying goes – although customers who had more important business were allowed inside the shop.

ROSE GARDEN

Japanese oasis set among the roses of Florence

Viale Giuseppe Poggi, 2
Admission free
Tel: 055 2625342
From mid-May to end of June, every day from 8am to 8pm
Undergoing restructuring to make it suitable for year-round opening
Only partially accessible to those with restricted mobility

One jewel box can enclose another. Although less famous than the iris garden alongside, the rose garden has the advantage of being open all year round, and of containing roses whose remarkable quality adds to the charm of the superb view of Florence to enjoy from here. The garden was designed by Giuseppe Poggi himself, on terraces laid out by Attilio Pucci for the cultivation of roses. Complete with the narrow winding paths that were such a feature of nineteenth-century romantic gardens – together with numerous belvederes from which to enjoy the view – this garden is on a sloping site that required the creation of a very special irrigation system, with water from a cistern in Piazzale Michelangelo being distributed throughout the garden by a number of different channels. This carefully designed system reveals the scientific precision that went into the design of the entire layout of a garden which now contains a thousand different species of plant – and more than three hundred varieties of rose. At the heart of this jewel box is another large-

ly unknown gem: a Japanese garden. This was the creation of the architect Yasuo Kitayama, working in collaboration with seven gardeners.

Inspired by the Zen principles of an oasis of *shorai-teien* (the future), the garden was laid out using materials imported directly from Japan in an act of homage to the Japanese city of Kyoto, which is twinned with Florence. Japanese monks from Kyoto's Kodai-ji Zen temple carried out a full ceremony of purification here in 2004, to mark the fortieth anniversary of the twinning of the two cities.

THE FLORENCE PRIZE EXHIBITION ㉓

Recreating in nature a flower invented for political reasons

Piazzale Michelangelo
Admission free
Open April 24 to May 20 (possible changes depending on which day national holiday of April 25 falls)
Opening hours: 10am to 12.30pm and 3pm to 7pm; the competition is judged in mid-May and the prizes presented at Palazzo Vecchio
Tel: 055 483112 • www.irisfirenze.it
Only partially accessible to those with restricted mobility

For centuries, Florence has been identified by a flag now seen all over the city and at all sorts of urban events. Now used as everything from a logo for local crafts to a crest for sports teams, that symbol is as famous as Venice's Lion of St Mark or Rome's She-Wolf, even if it is less "imaginary" in nature or narrative in content. The *fleur-de-lis* associated with Florence does not really recall a specific episode or historical event, but could be said to symbolise the sobriety and elegance that are so much a part of the local temperament.

This is why in 1954 the City Council gave the podere bastioni (bastion lands) to the left of Piazzale Michelangelo over to the Italian Iris Society, which (in 1957) opened here a sort of temple to *the fleur-de-lis* (or rather, the Iris), which can only be visited for the month of May, when the plants are in bloom, offering a spectacle of colours and scents.

What is less well-known is that the aim of the Premio Firenze which the Society of the Iris organises each year is to produce – through grafts and cross-breeding – a bloom that is close as possible to the famous Florence *fleur-de-lis*, whose particular red hue does not exist in nature. Indeed nobody has yet managed to obtain the desired colour, given that lilies (irises) tend to be either purple or white.

Originally, the Florence fleur-de-lis was white on a red background. The colour scheme was decided by the Ghibellines, who deliberately chose as their emblem a flower that grew wild in the Tuscan countryside. To mark their political opposition, the Guelphs therefore chose a red lily on a white background, and when they took power took this as the crest of the city. To keep both historical traditions satisfied, the Provincial Government of Florence – as opposed to the City Council – has as its emblem a flower that is half red against a white background and half white against a red background.

The Iris Garden competition is, therefore, unique in that it strives to recreate a flower that was originally invented for political reasons.

The sacred symbolism of the fleur-de-lis

The *fleur-de-lis* is symbolically linked to the iris and the *lily* (*Lilium*). According to Miranda Bruce-Mitford, Louis VII the Younger (1147) was the first king of France to adopt the iris as his emblem and use it as a seal for his letters patent (decrees). As the name Louis was then spelled Loys, it supposedly evolved to "*fleur-de-louis*", then "*fleur-de-lis*", its three petals representing Faith, Wisdom and Courage.

In reality, even if there is a strong resemblance between the iris and the *fleur-de-lis*, the French monarch merely adopted an ancient symbol of French heraldry. In AD 496, an angel purportedly appeared before Clotilda (wife of Clovis, king of the Francs) and offered her a lily, an event that influenced her conversion to Christianity. This miracle is also reminiscent of the story of the Virgin Mary, when the Angel Gabriel appeared to her, holding a lily, to tell her she was predestined to be the mother of the Saviour. This flower is also present in the iconography of Joseph, Christ's father, to designate him as the patriarch of the new Holy dynasty of divine royalty.

In 1125, the French flag (and coat of arms) depicted a field of *fleurs-de-lis*. It remained unchanged until the reign of Charles V (1364), who officially adopted the symbol to honour the Holy Trinity, thus deciding to reduce the number of flowers to three. The flower's three petals also referred to the Trinity.

The lily stylised as a *fleur-de-lis* is also a biblical plant associated with the emblem of King David as well as Jesus Christ ("consider the lilies of the field..." Matthew 6:28-29). It also appears in Egypt in association with the lotus flower, as well as in the Assyrian and Muslim cultures. It became an early symbol of power and sovereignty, and of the divine right of kings, also signifying the purity of body and soul. This is why the ancient kings of Europe were godly,

consecrated by the Divinity through sacerdotal authority. Thus, theoretically, they were to be fair, perfect and pure beings as the Virgin Mary had been, she who is the "Lily of the Annunciation and Submission" (*Ecce Ancila Domine*, "Here is the Servant of the Lord", as Luke the Apostle reveals), and patron saint of all royal power.

The lily thus replaced the iris, which explains why, in Spanish, *fleur-de-lis* becomes *flor del lírio*, and why the two flowers are symbolically associated with the same lily.

Botanically, the *fleur-de-lis* is neither an iris nor a lily. The iris (*Iris germanica*) is a plant of the Iridaceae family that originates in northern Europe. The more commonly known lily species (*Lilium pumilum, Lilium speciosum, Lilium candidum*) are members of the Liliaceae family that originates in Central Asia and Asia Minor.

The true *fleur-de-lis* belongs to neither the Iridaceae nor the Liliaceae family. It is the *Sprekelia formosissima*, a member of the Amaryllidaceae family that originates in Mexico and Guatemala. Known in other languages as the Aztec lily, the São Tiago lily, and the St James lily, Sprekelia formosissima is the only species of the genus. It was named in the eighteenth century by botanist Carl von Linné when he received a few bulbs from J. H. Van Sprekelsen, a German lawyer. The Spanish introduced the plant to Europe when they brought bulbs back from Mexico at the end of the sixteenth century.

BASILICA OF SAN MINIATO AL MONTE

San Miniato's zodiac

Via delle Porte Sante, 34 • Phenomenon can be viewed annually on June 21
Church open Monday–Saturday 9.30am-1pm and 3pm-7pm, Sunday 3pm-7pm

The marble zodiac on the floor of the basilica of San Miniato al Monte (St Minias on the Mountain) dates back to 1207 and was long regarded simply as a decorative motif modelled on the one in the Baptistery (no longer in use, see p. 88).

In 2011, however, meridian expert Simone Bartolini discovered that this zodiac was one of the oldest solstitial markers in Europe. Although there is abundant documentation on the Baptistery and the Duomo meridians, little was known about the one in San Miniato.

The phenomenon occurs only on June 21, but emotions run so high that it's worth planning a visit on that day. At 1.53 pm, close to solar noon, the sunray that penetrates through a small window to the right forms a sword of light that slowly but accurately comes to rest on the sign of Cancer (the zodiacal division that begins around the feast day of St John the Baptist, patron saint of Florence). After a few minutes, the ray moves on and the effect disappears. This brief moment reveals phenomena such as the movement of the Earth, the perfect synchronisation of this movement with the Sun, and the remarkable layout of the building that captures the summer solstice so precisely. Some even say that the venerable zodiac of San Miniato comes alive at that moment.

Thus the zodiac on the floor in front of the altar becomes the central element of an edifice that was built in order to respond to a precise relationship with the stars, confirming the link between medieval spirituality and oriental mysticism. Remember that St Minias was himself of Greek or Armenian origin.

Indeed the cult of the zodiac had Babylonian origins before Christianity appropriated it. The basilica of San Miniato is itself oriented from west to east, like many other churches until the end of the thirteenth century, to allow worshippers to pray facing east, just as the Cross of Calvary lay to the east. Moreover, this zodiac, with the phrase *haec est porta coeli* (this is the gate of heaven), invites further research on the true meaning of the various demons that adorn the mosaics of the basilica, or the Holy Grail painted on the vases above the doors.

The reverential atmosphere of San Miniato makes the phenomenon even more impressive than Toscanelli's "hole" in the cathedral (see p. 71).

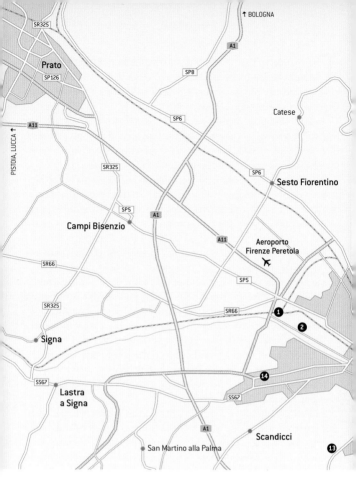

Outskirts of Florence

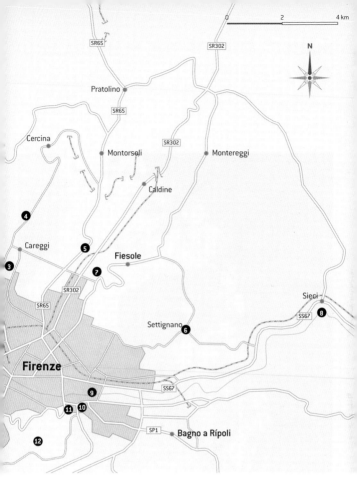

MAUSOLEUM OF THE MAHARAJA OF KOLHAPUR ①

A maharaja in Florence

Piazzaletto dell'Indiano

Although the whole city is familiar with this mausoleum, if only because the famous "Indian viaduct" (Viadotto dell'Indiano) is named after it, hardly any local people go there, and understandably very few tourists visit it either. To add to its interest, the place is off the beaten track, in the depths of the vast Cascine Park. You can reach it by two different routes, the easiest being to drive the length of the park as far as Piazzaletto dell'Indiano, at the western limits; the other is to follow Via Pistoiese, going under Ponte dell'Indiano, then on the left, take Via Piemonte and then the little tunnel under the railway lines and pass under the bridge again to finally reach Cascine, where you can park. A footbridge across the Mugnone waters takes you back to the Piazzaletto.

There you'll find an extraordinary funerary monument, erected by Charles Francesco Fuller in 1874: the statue of an elephant protected by a baldaquin which features a commemorative epigraph in Italian, reproduced in English, Hindi and Punjabi on the other three sides, the only public inscription in these Indian languages in Florence, at least to our knowledge.

A little contemporary house and some decorative features add to the picturesque air. It was here that Rajaram Chuttraputti, Maharaja of Kolhapur, was cremated in 1870 at only twenty years of age, having succumbed to a mysterious ailment on his return from England, in a hotel room at Piazza Ognissanti.

The painful demise of this charming Indian moved the whole city at the time, and cosmopolitan nineteenth-century Florence proved itself diplomatic enough to find a site to honour the remains of the young maharaja according to an age-old exotic ritual, to ease the departure of his soul thousands of kilometres from his native land. The convergence of two rivers, the Arno and the Mugnone, an auspicious site for a cremation in Brahmanic ritual, thus allowed tradition to be respected: the funeral cortege crossed Cascine Park and the ashes were scattered on the water.

Ever since, the "Indian" has been a popular character in Florence, even though many residents have now forgotten the story behind his name.

With its panoramic pedestrian crossing, the Ponte all'Indiano (Indiano Bridge) across the Arno was the world's first earth-anchored cable-stayed bridge. In other words, the suspended structure is supported only by the long steel cables, each with a span of over 200 metres.

Esoteric symbolism of Parco delle Cascine

Cascine Park was developed at the initiative of Cosimo I de' Medici from 1563. Originally, its structure and function were very different. It was a farming and hunting estate reserved for the Medici, specialising in cattle-breeding and cheese-making, hence the name Cascine, from *cascio* ("place where *cascio* – cheese – is produced").

Over the following centuries, the production of specialised crops and rare species of fruit trees gradually increased, but it wasn't until Medici rule ended in favour of the House of Lorraine that the park was opened to the public and its layout modified.

Following the interest of Grand Duke Ferdinand III (1769–1824), Cascine began to be filled with examples of neoclassical and neo-Egyptian architecture with highly symbolic forms and inscriptions.

The grand duke had, as it happened, joined the Freemasons and commissioned two court architects, Giuseppe Manetti and Gaspero Paoletti, to install an esoteric and initiatory journey through architectural features, buildings and groves, many traces of which still remain. Near the entrance to the modern Piazzale Vittorio Veneto are two fountains, one dedicated to Narcissus and the other to the winged horse Pegasus.

The first, which is pyramid-shaped, evokes the myth of Narcissus by inviting the visitor, before setting out on his itinerary of learning,

to look at himself, or rather to look within himself, to observe his deep nature, returning to the primordial waters that will allow him to be born again.

There is a plaque in honour of Percy Bysshe Shelley, who apparently was inspired by this place to write his *Ode to the West Wind* in 1820. The Pegasus fountain, a symbol of the victory of light over the obscurity of matter, is now missing its winged horse sculpture, which has been destroyed.

It evokes the Hippocrene spring on Mount Helicon in Greece, where Apollo and the Muses quenched their thirst from its alchemical waters.

Venturing further into the park, you'll discover a stone pyramid, an esoteric Masonic symbol that represents the union between Earth and Heaven. From a square base, where the number four represents the earthly dimension, unity is attained at the peak of the pyramid, in other words the divine dimension.

This pyramid also had a practical function: it was a cooler for preserving the victuals for the grand duke's court.

The initiatory route through the park is punctuated by various statues along tree-lined avenues, bearing other imposing symbols such as panthers and sphinxes, as well as bacchanalian images with Dionysian decorations.

You'll then discover the small neoclassical temples called *uccelliere* (aviaries) because they held birds; or *pavonières* (ornamental peacock cages), because they are decorated with friezes representing peacocks, symbols of rebirth. This route continues to Otto Viottole ("crossroads of the eight paths"), near Cornacchie ("crow") mead-

ow, the former hunting estate. Here a semicircular space opens out, divided into regular sections from which eight trails start, the figure eight symbolising the Infinite. The various paths indicate that only the initiate who has had access to the Knowledge will choose the path that leads to Heaven and Infinity.

MUSEO DELL'ISTITUTO AGRARIO ② (AGRICULTURAL SCHOOL MUSEUM)

Natural science treasures at Cascine

Viale delle Cascine, 11
Access on request if places are available, when the faculty is open, by calling 055 362 161 between 8am and 1pm, or faxing 055 360 003

Little known to Florentines and a real gem to specialists, the Istituto Tecnico Agrario Statale (State Agricultural Technical School), is the successor to the grandly named Regia Scuola Agraria di Pomologia e Orticoltura (Royal Agricultural School of Pomology and Horticulture), founded in 1882 in Cascine Park, near Le Pavoniere swimming pool.

Seriously damaged during the Second World War, then by the 1966 floods, but always rising from the ashes, this school was planned in an innovative way, with a stress on experiment and research. Thus major collections were put together here: botany (herbarium, superb reproductions of flowers and fungi), zoology (reptiles, invertebrates, mammals, amphibians); anatomy (reproductions of skeletons and bones); geology, mineralogy and even palaeontology (fossils from Tuscany), to which have been added several sets of plaster, resin or wax reproductions, genuine works of art.

The exhibition space also includes hundreds of devices used in physics, chemistry, agriculture, topography and meteorology, as well as a special attraction: a model showing the development of Italian overseas colonies.

Finally, the museum has greenhouses filled with rare plants, an interesting seed collection – notably olives – and a remarkable scientific library in which some volumes date back to the sixteenth century. In addition, the institution itself is continually enriched with important private collections of minerals, books, photographs, botanical specimens, and so on. It's a pity that this heritage is not displayed to its best advantage, but the reason why this collection has been relegated to the idiosyncratic category is probably the important legacy of the Renaissance and a culture not predisposed to science. We find this regrettable as a museum so varied and fascinating deserves far more than a quick visit.

ANATOMICAL MUSEUM
OF THE UNIVERSITY OF FLORENCE

A pedestal table made entirely of human organs

Viale Giovan Battista Morgagni 85, presso l'Auditorium Filippo Pacini
Tel: 055 2758050
Open Mon–Fri, by appointment

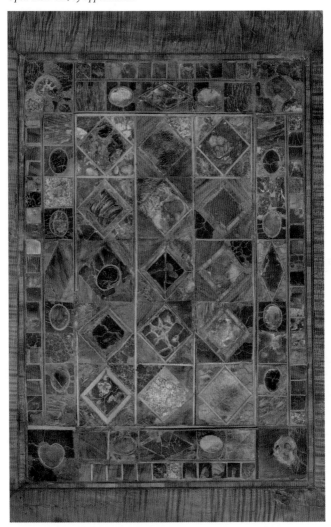

Every major institute of medicine has its own anatomical museum. Nevertheless, the one at the medical school of the University of Florence stands out, due to the unusual nature of its collection.

Its long display cases, aligned in a single vast room, contain an astonishing number of skulls and digestive systems of every size. You will also note a few especially remarkable heads, still covered with shiny skin. Although the eye sockets are vacant, the open mouths reveal perfect sets of teeth, and the veins and nerves still look quite lifelike. In the chiaroscuro, the aborted foetuses swimming in jars of formaldehyde look like monsters. However, some of them are still translucent, allowing you to inspect each of their internal organs. Another marvel is a skull sawn into three parts that fit together perfectly, with openings making it possible to observe the inside of the chamber. A set of male genitalia, of impressive size, is exhibited nearby, in a prominent position.

Not only is the visitor disconcerted to behold a gallery of human body parts; these fragments are preserved according to a unique process. The technique was invented by a character who was just as unique, Girolamo Segato (1792–1836). Unlike his colleagues, Segato was also an Egyptologist. He was especially intrigued by the pyramids (he spent three days in a row exploring the lightless caverns of the one at Saqqarah). The ingenious process whereby he conserved human viscera was based on mummification. It was called "petrification", although a more accurate term would be "mineralization", or fossilization. Segato alone knew the secret steps to achieve the desired effect: all of the organs to which the process was applied maintained their resilience and "living colour". The results were so striking that Segato was accused of dabbling in magic. Instead of revealing his technique, however, he resolved to destroy every trace of his method when he lost the financial support of the Grand Duke of Tuscany.

Despite the fact that Segato was ostracised while living, his own remains lie at the Basilica of Santa Croce, alongside those of national heroes like Galileo. Segato's tomb is ornamented with a plaque bearing these words: "Had his art not perished with him, the petrified body of Girolamo Segato of Belluno might be displayed here. He was an extraordinary specimen of the glory of human wisdom, and a more commonly observed example of a life of misery."

His masterpiece is doubtless his most macabre work. It is a pedestal table made of 214 carefully arranged fragments of petrified human organs. Some of them are still identifiable: here, a little kidney; there, a tiny kneecap, complete with meniscus. Segato made the table as a gift for the Grand Duke of Tuscany, who failed to appreciate it.

VILLA MEDICI CAREGGI

*House of Lorenzo the Magnificent
and the Neoplatonists*

Viale Pieraccini, 17
Tel: 055 4279755 or 055 4279080
Monday–Friday from 9am to 6pm, but we recommend afternoon visits
Admission free; booking required for groups

Although the Careggi villa and its grounds are located in a suburb on the outskirts of town, just after the Careggi hospital complex, this was the favourite residence of Lorenzo de' Medici (Lorenzo the Magnificent), the site of his death and of his Neoplatonic Academy, a philosophical and theological research and study centre unequalled in Europe. Far from the Florentine hurly-burly, outwith the tourist circuit, it is also a place of beauty and calm not to be missed. Inside these walls the Hebrew Kabbalah and the texts of Averroes, the Apocryphal Evangelists and the works of the philosophers of antiquity, like Plato and Plotinus, were studied, in search of a common source of human thought and spirituality. It was a fundamental attempt at synthesis and wisdom which, if it had been continued after Lorenzo's death, may have made it possible to avoid the schisms, wars, repression and persecution of religious minorities, and to spare Europe's destiny a great many trials. It is an extraordinary experience to visit what used to be the Laurentian headquarters, passing through the offices of the Azienda Sanitaria Locale (ASL, equivalent of Social Security) which are based here. To its credit, the ASL has opened to the public a group of buildings, certain parts of which are not lacking in charm, despite the many renovations over the centuries. The first includes a small lodge painted with frescoes which lends itself particularly well to the astronomical flights of fancy of Italian scholar Pico della Mirandola, a salon with a monumental fireplace and a large citrus glasshouse, not to mention the beautiful park, an ideal place for philosophical debates in the shade of the lush foliage.

Lorenzo il Magnifico: at the heart of Neoplatonism

Lorenzo de' Medici (Florence, January 1 1449 – Careggi, April 9 1492), as well as being a politician and statesman, was also a great patron and protector of scholars, writers, poets, artists and hermetists. A man who encouraged the development of Italy's first printing shops, he also nurtured the Renaissance humanism that rejected scholasticism in favour of an exploration of life that focused more upon humankind as the centre of the universe. Lorenzo the Magnificent was a particular supporter of the Neoplatonism whose relations with the hermetism of the day have long been accepted. It was under his protection, for example, that Marsilio Ficino translated the *Corpus Hermeticum* from Greek into Latin (published in Florence in 1471), as well as such works at the *Chaldean Oracles* and *Orphic Hymns*. Another eminent figure, Pico della Mirandola, dedicated himself entirely to the Christianisation of the Jewish Kabbalah, with the result that he was initially condemned by the Church and was only saved from these accusations of heresy by Lorenzo's intervention. His argument was that numerous monastic orders within Europe had engaged in the study of magic and astrology and that Pico della Mirandola's motivations had been purely scholarly. Fearing the power of the Florentine duke, the Church accepted this defence and there the matter came to an end. Others interested in Neoplatonism were the poets Pulci and Politien and such great artists as Botticelli and Ghirlandaio, while Michelangelo himself began his studies in a workshop under the patronage of Lorenzo il Magnifico.

Neoplatonic Academy

The importance and ambition of the Neoplatonic Academy are still not fully understood. Founded in Villa Careggi by the philosopher and theologician Marsilio Ficino in 1459, on the initiative of Cosimo de' Medici, its purpose was to study the great traditions of thinking and spirituality – Judaism and the Kabbalah, Christianity, Platonic and Plotinic philosophy, Pythagoras, Orphism, Hermes Trismegisto (see p. 198) and other sources of antiquity – in order to attain "theological peace". This field of esoteric study and research exalted the subject of personal freedom in the image of God, as marvellously expressed by Pico della Mirandola in *Oration on the Dignity of Man*: "We have given you, O Adam, no visage proper to yourself, nor endowment properly your own, in order that whatever place, whatever form, whatever gifts you may, with premeditation, select, these same you may have and possess through your own judgement and decision. The nature of all other creatures is defined and restricted within laws which We have laid down; you, by contrast, impeded by no such restrictions, may, by your own free will, to whose custody We have assigned you, trace for yourself the lineaments of your own nature. I have placed you at the very centre of the world, so that from that vantage point you may with greater ease glance round about you on all that the world contains. We have made you a creature neither of heaven nor of earth, neither mortal nor immortal, in order that you may, as the free and proud shaper of your own being, fashion yourself in the form you may prefer. It will be in your power to descend to the lower, brutish forms of life; you will be able, through your own decision, to rise again to the superior orders whose life is divine." Another extraordinary aspect of the Academy was its rapport with political power, first with Cosimo, then with Lorenzo the Magnificent. After the latter's death in 1492 and the Academy's move to the Oricellai gardens, their political relations continued with the republicans and anti-Medicians, not to mention Niccolò Machiavelli, among others. It went so far that the implication of some academicians in the conspiracy against Cardinal Giulio de' Medici in 1523 forced the institution to close. It was exactly this rapport with the powerful that made the ambitions of Florentine Neoplatonism pragmatic, to such an extent that Pico della Mirandola turned up in Rome to try to convince the papacy of an ecumenical theological vision in which Christianity should appear as the apogee of other traditions – Greek, Jewish and even Islamic – which had always been in communication thanks to common truths to which only initiates held the secrets. Inevitably, the Academy's ideas on beauty influenced the arts (da Vinci, Botticelli, Signorelli, Perugino and the Pollaiolo brothers, to name a few) because, for Marsilio Ficino, it was through the creative power of the imagination that the condition of humanity is revealed. Even the poetry of Lorenzo the Magnificent was motivated, like the works of Ange Politien, by the principles of affirmation of the will and the need to "seize the day", while studies on perspective by Leon Battista Alberti were also driven by the quest for the "third dimension", an "in-depth approach" typical of Neoplatonic man. The proportion of forms and the value of numbers, not only symbolic but revealing hidden truths – research similar to the Kabbalistic quest – constituted one of the esoteric itineraries of Florentine Neoplatonism, as an individual discipline to access a body of knowledge which, in a state of permanent tension between good and evil, vice and virtue, reason and obscurity, followed the absolute of True Ideas or Eternal Truths. Among the vast fields that the academicians researched can even be found one of the earliest gastronomic treatises, a work by Bartolomeo Sacchi (*alias* Platina): *On Honourable Pleasure and Health*. Published in 1474, the work not only included recipes, but also prescribed physical exercise and a suitable diet, while praising regional food. It is no surprise that this recipe book has now been republished (Éditions Einaudi), as a pioneer of *slow* food and the recommendation to eat local produce.

MONTERINALDI ARCHITECTURAL COMPLEX ⑤

The utopian experience of an ideal citadel

Via di Monterinaldi

I n the 1950s and 1960s, architect Leonardo Ricci and his colleagues Giovanni Klaus Koenig and Gianfranco Petrelli built a utopian citadel consisting of about twenty villas, directly inspired by the work of Frank Lloyd Wright, on the slopes of Monterinaldi. For Ricci, Monterinaldi with its panoramic views of both Fiesole and Florence was a practical attempt to create an ideal "theoretical house", not standing alone but perfectly assimilated with its environment and harmoniously integrated with its neighbours. He envisaged a proper community with shared projects and aesthetic values, and a communal organisation. To reach the site, you

climb up the narrow lanes just above Via Bolognese. You then arrive at a homogeneous complex of charming residences which, even from the outside, blend into the surrounding landscape in remarkably innovative ways, experimenting with shapes and construction materials. All the roofs are accessible and have been transformed into panoramic terraces. The exterior walls are often sloping, built from regional stone in the style of medieval ramparts, and sometimes one house is joined to another. The last house was completed in 1968, but the plans also included some common spaces – open workshops, swimming pool, kindergarten – to create a communal spirit among the various residents, including many former artists, some of whom were still working at the time.

Monterinaldi, sometimes referred to as the "Martians' village" but widely admired as one of the most ambitious architectural complexes of its time, is the result of a conception of habitat that had gained a following. It exemplifies a successful if unique attempt to achieve a kind of urban utopia at the gates of Florence.

VILLA GAMBERAIA

(6)

Florentine villa *par excellence*

Via del Rossellino, 72
www.villagamberaia.it
Visit the gardens daily from 9am to 5pm in winter and 9am to 6pm in summer
Booking recommended, particularly at the weekend
Admission: e10 (full price); € 8 (concessions); public holidays and preceding day: € 12
The interior of the villa can be viewed by groups of at least ten for a supplement
of € 5 per person
Tel: 055 697205, or e-mail villagam@tin.it
Telefono: 055 697205, o scrivere a villagam@tin.it

The sumptuous Villa Gamberaia de Settignano, by which there once flowed a stream famed for its crayfish (hence its name, from gambero di fiume, crayfish), has a history which is unforgettable to say the least. It was built by an ancestor of the sculptor Rossellino and belonged, among others, to the illustrious Capponi family, then at the end of the nineteenth century to Princess Giovanna Ghykha, sister of Queen Natalie of Serbia, before being bought by Baron von Ketteler. After the Second World War, it was taken over by the Vatican, and finally in 1952 by Marcello and Nerina Marchi. Over the centuries, each owner left their mark, leading to the current development which sets off the park. The villa complex has been transformed into tourist accomodation and facilities for ceremonies and seminars.

The view of Florence is worth a detour: a stretch of pink roofs along the banks of the Arno, from which the Brunelleschi cupola emerges with the Amennines in the background. The park itself includes two elegant monumental gardens graced with ornamental ponds and geometrical alleys, rows of cypress trees, a grove of holm oaks and a bowling green. Enough delights to wander among open-mouthed in a labyrinth enriched with flights of steps, passages, fountains – an ideal place for touring Shakespeare plays or for playing hide and seek or blind man's buff. With its two magnificent salons and interior courtyard surrounded by arcades, the villa equals the gardens. But its most beautiful aspect is incontestably the apartments in the seventeenth-century former chapel and a fourteenth-century country house converted into a lemon press. They do credit to the canon of Tuscan interiors: large fireplaces, exposed beams and box ceilings, brick floors, period furniture – and the unmissable view over Florence. You'll be loath to leave.

NEARBY ⑦
Cantina Guidi ceramics
Via Pagnini, 22r • Tel: 055 480205

Opened in 1946, this wine merchant's (cantina) was one of the first specialist food shops in Florence. Although now closed, the original façade covered with Art Nouveau panels, the work of a great Italian ceramist, Antonio Chini, has become an object of curiosity.

The Chini were a family dynasty of Art Nouveau architects and decorators, whose work features in houses and chapels along the main roads of their native village of Borgo San Lorenzo, in the Mugello district. Their work can of course also be seen at Villa Pecori Giraldi, where a large museum is dedicated to the Chini.

COMPLEX OF GUALCHIERE DI REMOLE

Treasure of industrial archaeology

Left bank of the Arno, along the SP34 secondary road linking Florence and Rosano, around 9 km from Viale Europa

Shortly after leaving the city, on the road leading to Rosano, you can still see a textile factory on the banks of the Arno, whose waters it formerly used. The original woollen mill that was set up after the 1333 floods stayed in production for centuries. It belonged to the Albizi family until 1541, then to Arte della Lana, one of the seven Florentine arts and crafts guilds, and later to the Florence Chamber of Commerce. This factory, an authentic monument to the culture of technology, thus shaped over the centuries the urban identity of the cradle of the Renaissance in the arts. Moreover, it bears witness to the organic and economic rapport that the city has always had with its river, which alone might make you curious to visit the Gualchiere complex, a still impressive industrial site where you can see the château-like structure with its mills and hydraulic wheels. The complex extends over 4,000 square metres, a large part of which is now in ruins, although there is a restoration project to use it as the headquarters of the International Centre for Traditional Knowledge (but there has also been talk in recent years of a hotel complex). On the initiative of UNESCO, the aim of this centre will be to promote and disseminate knowledge of traditional techniques, as well as the recovery and safeguarding of popular scientific culture. Today, left to its own devices, the former complex is a treasure of industrial archaeology at the very gates of Florence. This treasure is unique in Europe not only because of its equipment but also because of its medieval origins, even though it has been converted more than once, let alone its fundamental role in the organic rapport that human labour has always held with the river. In addition, for centuries Gualchiere was linked to the Sieci district, on the opposite bank of the Arno, by a ferry service. This forgotten site, unsuspected from the road, is not without charm, and neither is the short walk that takes you back to the tranquil and well-maintained banks of the Arno.

Gualchiere: a genuine "exclave" in Florence

Gualchiere holds another secret, another reason why this site merits a place in a guide to Florence: although the complex lies within the territory of the municipality of Bagno at Ripoli, it belongs to the municipality of Florence, so it is a genuine (and unusual) "exclave".

BRUNELLESCHI'S DOME IN MINIATURE ⑨

Architect's secrets revealed in an open-air laboratory

Parco dell'Anconella
Beside Via di Villamagna

Brunelleschi's dome has always been a puzzle if you consider the technical principles according to which it was designed and built. As an architectural feat it was certainly ahead of its time, but when scaffolding was recently erected in order to restore the fresco on the inner vault of the dome, a number of complex issues were revealed. Theories abounded on the possible solutions that architectural genius Brunelleschi might have used, until it was finally decided not only to use the occasion to draw up a detailed description of his dome but also to build a copy and thus reveal its secrets. So in 2007 a reproduction of the cathedral dome was built in Anconella Park on a scale of 1:5. The project, originally conceived by Italian architect Giovanni Michelucci, was implemented by Massimo Ricci, a noted expert on Brunelleschi's masterpiece.

The large-scale model systematically reproduces the structure of each brick, also on a scale of 1:5, set at an angle parallel to the surface of the vaulting rather than in a circular arrangement.

Ricci discovered how the structure of the dome was built up through a succession of horizontal radial mouldings: the Anconella model is a real open-air laboratory that throws light on Brunelleschi's secrets.

This mini-dome has been left two-thirds complete so that the interior structure can be seen. Moreover, the builders experimented with the techniques and equipment of the time, such as cables, pulleys and movable ribs as supports.

NINFEO DEL GIOVANNOZZI

Surprising grotto at Gavinana

Via del Paradiso, 5
To arrange a free visit, call Mr Vangelisti (owner) at 347 796 2509

In the Florentine suburbs near Gavinana there is a private garden with a hidden grotto built in an eccentric style that forms part of Villa del Bandino, later inherited by the Niccolini family. It was the Niccolinis who in 1746 commissioned the painter and sculptor Giuseppe Giovannozzi da Settignano to build a "nymphaeum", a sanctuary consecrated to water nymphs, a rustic construction with three arches topped with ornamental vases and decorated with rich Baroque mosaics encrusted with shells.

All this shows that Giovannozzi took pleasure in creating this architectural diversion, which he built himself with the help of his son and a workman. In the grotto you'll find a number of benches and notably the pool, which used to be fitted with intermittent jets of water linked to the Bigallo wells.

In the centre rose the statue of Venus, which was stolen during the First World War and never heard of again. Its presence was more than justified among the coloured pebbles of the grotto because the goddess of Love presided over this sanctuary, which not only served as an imaginative refuge from the heat, or an unusual setting for fêtes or al fresco refreshments, but could also be used as a natural boudoir for courting couples.

The nymphaeum has its roots far from Boboli or Villa Demidoff, but it has the same "rocky" spirit that dares and defies the commonplace,

not afraid of ridicule but on the contrary giving free rein to the imagination, a witness to a carefree Florence. Recently restored by scrupulous owners and developed a few years ago as a unique setting for theatrical performance, the nymphaeum is now set in a simple green space overlooked by some modern buildings, as if playing hide and seek in the beautiful panorama surrounding it.

CANTO DEGLI ARETINI

⑪

Former communal grave, enclave of Arezzo

Via di Ripoli, 51, at the corner of Via Benedetto Accolti

The phrase *canto degli Aretini* ("the Aretini corner") can lead to confusion because canto also means "song" in Italian. But you won't find anything particularly musical at this corner of Via di Ripoli, which forms a strange sort of enclave: this tiny part of Florence, as announced on a column surrounded by a guardrail, is actually administered by the city of Arezzo, as the inscription on the plaque recalls – QUESTO COSIDDETTO CANTONE DI AREZZO CHE È DEL COMUNE GHIBELLINO PROPRIETÀ – which goes on to evoke the "MEMORIA DEGLI INFAUSTI ODII DA CITTÀ A CITTÀ OGGI NELL'ITALIANA CONCORDE POTENZA ABOLITI PER SEMPRE".* This "*canto*" marks the burial place of several hundred Aretini who had died in Florentine prisons. They were the poorest among 1,000 soldiers that the Florentines took prisoner in 1189, at the end of the battle of Campaldino. Most of them were freed shortly afterwards, following the payment of a ransom, but the others stayed in their dungeon where they soon perished. Their memory has been perpetuated in this little patch of ground under the care of the curiously extra-communal administration of the city of Arezzo, which on June 11 each year places a floral wreath there at the same time as the Municipality of Florence.

FONDAZIONE SPADOLINI NUOVA ANTOLOGIA

Villa Il Tondo dei Cipressi *(The Circle of Cypresses)*

Via Pian dei Giullari, 36a
Tel: 055 2336071
Open Monday–Wednesday 9am-6pm, Tuesday and Thursday 9am-5pm
Fondazione Spadolini Nuova Antologia
Villa Il Tondo dei Cipressi (The Circle of Cypresses)
Via Pian dei Giullari, 139
Visits by appointment
Tel: 055 687 521

With its library of 100,000 volumes, the Spadolini Foundation is also home to one of the largest and oldest Italian cultural magazines, the *Nuova Antologia*, the first issue of which was published in 1866. However, it is mainly a monument to Giovanni Spadolini, historian, long-time secretary of the Italian Republican Party, and leader of Italy's first non-Christian Democratic government. In the foundation's two buildings on the beautiful hill of Pian dei Giullari, you can stroll through European history, particularly the Risorgimento, in an inspiring but scientific atmosphere where no detail has been overlooked In some respects, the secular climate of Florence – a city unwilling to go over the top but always sustained by its faith in reason and a strong civic culture – can still be felt today in Spadolini's library and former residence. From its headquarters, the foundation organises a wide range of activities, from scholarships to research projects; it is also used as a congress venue. Various collections can be consulted in the library (temporary exhibitions are also held here). In the main building, you can immerse yourself in the world of Spadolini the politician. With an intellectual curiosity worthy of the Renaissance, Spadolini was just as interested in the figurative arts as in historical relics and antique books, and he collected minor works of art, with a predilection for the Risorgimento. You'll find contemporary portraits of Garibaldi, Mazzini and Cavour, paintings by Neapolitan artists and works by the Macchiaioli group of nineteenth-century Florentine artists, as well as works by such twentieth-century painters as Primo Conti, Renato Guttuso, Giorgio Morandi, Ardengo Soffici, Ottone Rosai and of course Spadolini's father Guido, who passed on his love of painting to his son. The events that marked Italy in the twentieth century are interspersed with caricatures by Longanesi and Maccari, along with hundreds of prints and drawings. There is also a collection of awards and gifts presented to Spadolini – by Margaret Thatcher and Konstantinos Karamanlis (prime ministers of the UK and Greece respectively), for example, and a number of international universities – throughout his long career as head of state, minister and president of the Senate. Under its able director, the historian Cosimo Ceccuti, the foundation's two buildings form a unique site. On the one hand, they are the repositories of the history of a great tradition starting with the Risorgimento and ending in republicanism. On the other (unlike a traditional museum), they show the permanent effect of this thinking on politics and contemporary society.

NEARBY

Villa Il Tasso plaque

Outside the villa Il Tasso (30 Via Benedetto Fortini), right next to the gateway, a stone plaque dating from 1704 indicates the distance from the city centre. Farther along this same street, among the ancient graffiti on the wall around the villa, you'll find an 1830 frieze.

CIMITERO ALLORI

Non-Catholic cemetery

Via Senese, 184
Open October 1–March 31 from 8am to 12.30pm and 2.30pm to 5pm,
and April 1–September 30 8am to 12pm and 3pm to 6pm; closed Sunday

On the southern outskirts of Florence, in the suburb of Galluzzo, the little cemetery of the Allori ("laurels") is a haven of eternal peace whose history is little known. Although it is not exactly a monumental burial ground, from an artistic point of view there are several interesting tombs that give a certain cohesion to an otherwise rather eclectic place. Besides, the surrounding countryside is fairly typical of the Florentine landscape, which has had to adapt to the vagaries of the road network, such as the petrol stations and the often heavy traffic. The site nevertheless complies well with the new norms which, in the nineteenth century, led to the closure of the English cemetery at Piazza Donatello and the removal of most cemeteries outside the city. The Allori cemetery was opened to cater to Florentine residents who were non-Catholics: Protestant, Orthodox, atheist and even Jews and Muslims. Thus you'll discover among the tombs unusual sectors of Florentine society: the evangelical and English communities, and even some Russian aristocrats. The variety illustrates the diverse characters who have been buried here, from the British historian and writer Harold Acton to the antiquarian Frederick Stibbert, the Swiss painter Arnold Böcklin, or that magnificent and controversial writer Oriana Fallaci, who was very proud of his Florentine identity. This diversity came from the Protestant community, whose deceased were laid to rest in the Swiss or "English" cemetery of Piazza Donatello. When major works were undertaken in order to turn Florence into the capital of the Kingdom of Italy from 1865 to 1870, the ramparts were demolished and the English cemetery found itself not only in the urban area but encircled by roads. It was at that time that the Allori cemetery was established, in 1860, in the Galluzzo district: the last resting-place with its simple gateway for all those who could not or would not be buried in Catholic ground.

GIARDINO DI ARCHIMEDE (14)

Incredible museum for playing with numbers

Museum of Mathematics
Via san Bartolo a Cintoia, 19
Tel: 055 7879594, open Monday–Friday from 9am to 1pm and Sunday 3pm to
7pm (closed August and public holidays)

In the suburbs of Florence you might suddenly notice an unusual house equipped with strange aerial walkways and striking tilted features, architecture which is bizarre to say the least and out of place in the sober urban uniformity. This curious building is home to a museum known particularly to schools, as there is no equivalent in Italy and perhaps not in the whole of Europe. The museum is the result of an innovative and ambitious project: to familiarise the general public with mathematics by offering entertainment and interactive participation, in order to arouse their curiosity about numbers and shapes. As we are in Tuscany, the museum had to begin with a programme dedicated to the mathematician Leonardo Fibonacci, also known as Leonardo of Pisa, author of the "golden laws" on the numerical structure of nature, as well as the famous *Liber Abaci* (*Book of Calculation*, 1202), a cornerstone in the transmission of medieval mathematical sciences to the West. However, the historical approach is only part of this museum, which includes an interactive section on Pythagoras' theorem, explored through a series of puzzles, while the section entitled *Oltre il compasso, la geometria delle curve* (Beyond the compass, the geometry of curves) reprises and expands on a successful exhibition of the 1990s, devoted to geometry and organised entirely around games and interactive experiences. Besides these permanent features, the museum offers temporary exhibitions and a series of recreational workshops on the practical applications of mathematics: you can for example learn how to fold paper into special shapes, let yourself be seduced by fascinating musical exercises, or count like the Sumerians. If you're looking for an unusual museum, you'll find it here, all the more so as Florentine museums are often conservative places, and almost all are in the city centre, whereas here for once the suburbs come into their own.

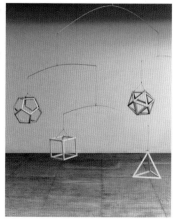

ALPHABETICAL INDEX

PHOTOGRAPHY CREDITS

All photos were taken by **Waris Grifi** with the exception of:

pages 70, 72, 89: **Carlo Caselli**
pages 48, 50, 92, 161, 198, 210, 211, 240, 268, 271: **DR**
pages 30: **Associazione dei Renaioli**
pages 196, 197, 272: **VMA**
page 123: **Libreria Antiquaria Gonnelli**
pages 230, 231, 232, 233: **Saulo Bambi - Museo di Storia Naturale/Firenze**
pages 120, 136, 137, 148, 149, 168, 169, 174, 260, 261, 274, 277: **Sailko**

The following texts were written by:
VMA: pages 13, 14, 15, 48, 49, 50, 51, 194, 195, 240, 241, 252, 253
Giacomo Bei: pages 30, 115
Roberto di Ferdinando: pages 28, 29, 32, 33, 65, 185, 220, 224, 225, 260, 261

Maps: **Cyrille Suss** - Layout Design: **Coralie Cintrat** - Layout: **Iperbole** - English Translation: **Jeremy Scott** - English Editing: **Kimberly Bess and Caroline Lawrence**

© JONGLEZ 2017
Registration of copyright: May 2017 – Edition: 03
ISBN: 978-2-36195-174-0
Printed in Bulgaria by Multiprint